THE ILLUSTRATED GUIDE TO

NATIVE AMERICAN

MYTHS AND LEGENDS

THE ILLUSTRATED GUIDE TO
NATIVE AMERICAN
MYTHS AND LEGENDS

LEWIS SPENCE

Introduced by
ARTHUR COTTERELL

LONGMEADOW
PRESS

Haida rattle (above) in the form of a head. Such rattles were used in most shamanistic rituals and dances of the Haida, who lived in the Queen Charlotte Islands, British Columbia. (Private collection.)

Mouth of the Fox River (frontispiece), Illinois, by Karl Bodmer. (Illustration from M. A. P. Wied-Neuwied, *Voyage dans l'intérieur de l'Amérique du Nord,* 1840–43.)

Research and additional text by Christine O'Brien
Picture research by Susan Rose-Smith
Design by Martin Lovelock

Library of Congress Cataloging-in-Publication Data
ISBN: 0-681-45400-8

Printed in Singapore

First Longmeadow Press Edition

0 9 8 7 6 5 4 3 2 1

CONTENTS

INTRODUCTION

Until the early seventeenth century, North America was inhabited solely by tribes who had migrated from the Asian world. The first inhabitants had crossed from Siberia to Alaska over a temporary land link towards the end of the Ice Age. Large-scale movements of people seem to have stopped when the glaciers shrank and the sea level rose, bringing the Bering Straits into being once more. Some contact between the Asian and North American continents probably continued intermittently down the millennia. The ancestors of the Athapascan-speaking tribes may not have arrived until only 3000 years ago, or even, as has been suggested, as recently as the 13th century, when Asia was dominated by the Mongols under Genghis Khan, with North America offering a safe haven. This theory is not universally accepted; however, little is known about the history of the settlement and migration of the ancestors of present-day Indian tribes.

The historical connection between East Asia and North America is most obvious in the respect paid to the *shaman*, or medicine man. On both sides of the Bering Straits, shamans acted as intermediaries between the spirit world and that of the human. Among the North American peoples, their area of responsibility encompassed the skills of the priest, prophet and physician. However, they were not formally instructed in a body of lore, but acquired their powers individually. Even in long-established tribal rituals, shamans were able to vary details as the spirit moved them. While in a trance, they could raise themselves to the upperworld where the spirits dwelled, thereby controlling the spirits of disease in order to exorcize them from the sick person. According to southeastern tribes like the Cree, Seminole and Shawnee, illness was derived from the presence of some harmful substance usually placed in the victim's body by the offended animal spirit. Once the medicine man had diagnosed the problem, special songs were sung to deal with the spirit, and medicinal herbs were administered to the sufferer. Another insight gained by the medicine man on an upperworld journey was the course of certain future events, hence the importance attached by many tribes to prophecy.

Great Mound at Grave Creek, Virginia. The mound-building peoples of North America flourished for over two millennia in an area from the Great Lakes in the north to the Gulf of Mexico in the south.

Apaches story-telling (opposite). Without a written language, the Native Americans transmitted their myths and legends orally. (Illustration from Edward Curtis, *The North American Indian*, 1907–30.)

The Chiricahua Mountains in Arizona were believed by the Apaches living nearby to be the home of mountain spirits who could cure illness.

A shaman, as seen through European eyes. The spirituality of the Native Americans was imperfectly understood by Christian settlers.

A Zuni woman. The complex ceremonial life of the Zuni people was organized by priests, medicine societies and matrilinear clans. (Illustration from Edward Curtis, *The North American Indian*, 1907–30.)

On earth the medicine man might also have been expected to consecrate territory; for example, to ensure that a village was correctly placed at the centre of the tribal world. For the Zuni of Arizona and New Mexico, the medicine man would have been following the great example of Po-shai-an-K'ia, the father of "medicine". This cultural hero and deity was originally the wisest of men, who interceded on behalf of a semi-formed creation with the sun god Awonawilona. Po-shai-an-K'ia had forced his way upward from the primordial slime in which Awonawilona created animals and men in subterranean caves. On the shores of a great ocean he persuaded the sun god to open a passage through which creation could emerge into the light. But to his horror, Po-shai-an-K'ia found that adaptation to underground living had engendered a chronic fear of the sun, so he set about acclimating every creature to its place in the world. During this work he founded the Zuni. This tribe belongs to the Pueblo Indian group. (The term 'Pueblo Indian' is generic, describing those tribes which inhabited *pueblos*, or permanent villages of brick, earth, clay and stone construction.)

Another of the Pueblo group claims a similar founder who travelled from one village to another, making sure each one was correctly sited.

The Pueblo Indians had permanent settlements of rammed-earth or stone construction, in a striking contrast to the wigwams and tepees of the Great Plains tribes. Yet records show that tribal lands were regarded as no less sacred by those hunters who followed the seasonal movements of game. The Sioux and the Arapahe had elaborate ceremonies for the cutting and sewing of a tent, as well as its placement on the ground. Long after the removal of these tribes to reservations, there are still echoes of the religious anxiety that accompanied the forcible clearances. The vehemence of recent Cree protests in Ontario and Quebec against proposals for hydro-electric schemes should be understood not only as a protest against ecological damage but also in the context of the desecration of ancestral sites.

In the seventeenth century, when systematic settlement of North

America from Europe was beginning, there existed more than 2000 separate Indian tribes. As many of these peoples were enemies, there was almost no possibility of their creating a united front against the incoming European. Yet the sheer force of European arms put the Indians at a permanent disadvantage. The Great Plains tribes took readily to horses and rifles, becoming a formidable foe, but serious resistance to the westward movement of settlers was always restricted to sparsely populated states. Indian casualties in battle were dwarfed by deaths resulting from previously unknown diseases. Smallpox, for example, wiped out whole tribes or forced the survivors to amalgamate like the Mandan and the Hidatsa, two peoples of Siouan stock now living on a reservation in North Dakota. The end of Indian North America was sealed by the policy of concentration in such areas, which began towards the close of the nineteenth century. Today there are some 3000 Federal Indian reservations in the USA. The surviving tribes which are not farmers have seen the greatest changes in their way of life. The great herds of buffalo have been slaughtered and the modern native Indian descendants of the buffalo hunters use the local supermarkets like any other North American group.

Study of their myths and legends reveals underlying similarities of belief. Nearly all their tales reaffirm tribal identity. When taboos are broken or customs patently ignored, the offender cannot avoid retribution, often by the agency of a spirit. On the other hand, the adventurous warrior can expect help from spirits, providing he is both courageous and courteous. Thus the young Sioux hero of the Snake-Ogre story even receives assistance from the monster's wife. Not only does she provide him with a magic pair of moccasins for his escape, but she also accepts death herself as the price of this aid. Moreover, other animal spirits contribute to the Snake's confusion during the pursuit. Little Toad, Muskrat, Turtle and Frog all side with handsome young Sioux.

Certain animal spirits are less straightforward in their dealings with the human race. One such spirit is Coyote, the mischievous trickster spirit of the Californian tribes. According to the Maidu Indians, Coyote pushed

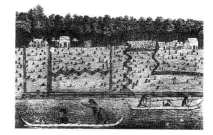

An American New Cleared Farm, showing cooperation between European settlers and Native Americans. (The Library Company of Philadelphia.)

Newspaper Rock, Canyonlands, Utah. Petroglyphs, symbols painted or carved on rocks, are found all over North America and may have marked sacred sites.

aside their creator deity not because he was better or stronger, but because men preferred to follow him. Although Coyote's actions are often monstrous and unnerving, he is not always aware of the havoc he introduces into the world. His ambiguous nature is transparent in a Maidu creation myth, where Coyote copied things with unfortunate results. Trying to make people as well, he laughed – and they were found to have only glass eyes. Later he tried to add to the order of creation, but his gifts turned out to be sickness, sorrow and death. Coyote was not unhappy when his own son died, possibly because he imagined he could revive the corpse by submerging it in a lake, a method of revivication already taught to the humans by the Maidu creator god. As his son remained lifeless, Coyote simply left the corpse to rot.

Mysterious deities such as Coyote gain perspective when it is realized that the North American peoples believed that animals were the original inhabitants of the continent, and that they were by no means inferior to human beings. Just as Coyote is the annoying opposite of the Maidu creator god, we find in "Algonquian Myths" another rivalry between two wolves, Malsum and his brother Glooskap, whose name means "the liar". In spite of his name, however, it is not the cunning Glooskap who represents evil. The Algonquian trickster god used his abilities to combat the bad designs that Malsum once had on the human beings. Out of exasperation, Glooskap killed Malsum and then battled against the fearful monsters who terrorized creation following his brother's death. Having overcome them, he decided it was time to return to the upperworld. When the appointed day arrived, Glooskap gave an enormous feast for all the animals on the shore of the lake, then drifted away in his canoe. A strange thing occurred when the god had disappeared from sight: the animals were dumbfounded to discover they could no longer communicate with each other.

Hein-mot Too-ya-la-kekt, known as Chief Joseph, of the Nez Percé, led his people in an unsuccessful bid for freedom from European occupation. (Illustration from Edward Curtis, *The North American Indian*, 1907–30.)

Coyote was said by Paiute legend to have turned animals that looked like people into these rocks at Bryce Canyon, Utah.

Lake Itasca, the source of the Mississippi in Minnesota, lies in the heart of the area occupied by peoples speaking languages of the Algonquian group.

Beavers at work. Valuable both for its fur and for its fatty meat, the beaver figures in many Native American legends. (Mansell Collection.)

The Algonquian-speaking tribes of the forest and plains – the Delaware, Fox, Miami, Powhatan and Blackfeet among others – believed that Glooskap would one day return and revive a golden age on earth. He is not the only New World hero to parallel the Celtic ruler, once-and-future king Arthur. In Mexico there survives the story of Quetzalcoatl, the snake-bird god, who sailed away on a raft of serpents to an enchanted land. On his arrival in 1519 the Spanish conquerer Hernando Cortés began a rumour that Quetzalcoatl had returned with his expedition to reclaim his throne from the Aztecs. The propaganda seems to have deeply disturbed the Aztec emperor Montezuma.

Belief in a renewed earth for the North American peoples was certainly part of the inspiration for the widespread Ghost Dance movement, a late nineteenth century messianic cult of the dead. The Ghost Dance had several precursors, including the teachings of great Shawnee medicine man Tenskwatawa. Around 1805 he announced the coming of a new world to the southeastern tribes. As a means of escape from the progressively deteriorating conditions in which the Indians found themselves forced to live, the Ghost Dance had considerable attraction. The message of Jack Wilson (also known as Wovoka), a Paiute, therefore spread quickly through the tribes living on reservations in Nevada, Wyoming, Oklahoma and Kansas. The son of a medicine man who had already developed a dance, Wovoka in 1889 foretold a day when all Indians, dead and alive, would be reunited in a regenerated world free from sorrow, diease and death. Through dancing, his followers were able to anticipate this blessed state and communicate with their dead relations. People of all ages joined in a dance which ended in rigidity and unconsciousness. The Navajo were proof against its blandishments, because they have lacked any belief in a glorious afterlife, as well as having a horror of the dead.

Possibly the greatest of the North American prophets was the legendary Hiawatha, whose name is variously translated as "he who makes rivers" and "he who seeks the wampum-belt". This chief is credited with a vision that led to the unification of several feuding tribes around the Great Lakes. The traditional date for the event was 1570. A leader of either the Mohawk or Onondaga tribe, Hiawatha was so horrified by the

Hiawatha, a sixteenth-century leader said to have found the Iroquois League, has become widely known as the subject of an epic poem by Longfellow.

slaughter caused by the apparently endless conflict between Iroquoian-speaking peoples that he called asssemblies to consider a peace plan. Eventually his persistence paid off, and the Five Nations agreed to settle old differences amicably. Most important of all, the tribal chiefs introduced a stringent regulation of the blood feud, without doubt the most common reason for inter-tribal wars.

However, the new confederacy of the Mohawk, Oneida, Onondaga, Cayuga and Seneca did not include every Iroquoian tribe. The particular enemy against whom it was intended to guarantee mutual support, the Hurons, actually spoke the same tongue. Though this means that Hiawatha only succeeded in reducing the scale of conflict rather than uniting all the Iroquois, the Five Nations he managed to bring together were able to exercise a positive influence for peace. An ally in this rare initiative was Dekanawida, a Mohawk chief. Possibly because his word was so respected in the tribal councils, a typical cluster of hero legends soon became attached to Dekanawida's name, which means "two river currents flowing together". One story would even make him a Huron, whose mother tried three times to drown him through a hole in the ice. The woman had been driven to this desperate measure by an omen which foretold calamity for the Hurons from his actions later in life. Three times she woke up next morning and found Dekanawida safe in her arms. That he was not a Mohawk is suggested by the manner of his investiture as chief. After the formation of the Five Nation confederacy, he was able to forbid the unnecessary appointment of a successor for the Mohawks on the grounds that no one could achieve more than he had done. Chosen for the chieftainship by merit, Dekananwida used his personal eminence to persuade the tribe to sink its identity into a larger group.

How difficult such a piece of diplomacy must have been to accomplish can be judged from the tale entitled "Promise of Vengeance". It concerns the capture of a Seneca boy by the Algonquian-speaking Illinois; his immediate vow of revenge; the inner determination that kept him a Seneca despite a testing stay with his captors; his eventual appointment as an Illinois war-leader against his own people; and the disaster he cunningly contrived for the war band he was supposed to lead to victory. Following the slaughter of the Illinois, the Senecas bore the exiled brave home in triumph, where he related "the story of his capture and long-meditated revenge. He became a great chief among his people, and even to this day his name is uttered by them with honour and reverence." Here in its most obvious form is the essence of North American Indian myth – the celebration of tribal identity.

Prehistoric Anasazi and Fremont peoples lived in this area of the Southwest, which is now the Arches National Park of Utah. The word "Anasazi" is Navajo for "The Old Ones".

Peyote drummer. An attempt to re-establish traditional Native American values, the peyote rite provoked opposition from the government in the late nineteenth century. (Illustration from Edward Curtis, *The North American Indian*, 1907–30.)

CHAPTER 1

ALGONQUIAN MYTHS AND LEGENDS

Glooskap and his brother Malsum, the Wolf, were twins. Their mother died at their birth, and out of her body Glooskap formed the sun and moon, animals, fishes, and the human race, while the malicious Malsum made mountains, valleys, serpents and every manner of thing which he considered would inconvenience the race of men.

Each of the brothers possessed a secret as to what would kill him. Malsum asked Glooskap in what manner he could be killed, and the elder brother, to try his sincerity, replied that the only way in which his life could be taken was by the touch of an owl's feather, or by that of a flowering rush. Malsum in his turn confided to Glooskap that he could only perish by a blow from a fern-root. The malicious Wolf, taking his bow, brought down an owl, and while Glooskap slept his brother struck him with a feather plucked from its wing. Glooskap immediately expired but to Malsum's chagrin came to life again.

Malsum resolved to learn his brother's secret and to destroy him at the first opportunity. Glooskap had told him, after his first attempt, that only a pine-root could kill him, and with this Malsum struck him while he slept as before. But Glooskap, rising up and laughing, drove Malsum into the forest and seated himself by a stream, where he murmured, as if musing to himself: "Only a flowering rush can kill me." Now he said this because he knew that Quah-beet, the Great Beaver, was hidden among the rushes on the bank of the stream and would hear every word he uttered. The Beaver went at once to Malsum and told him what he regarded as his brother's vital secret. The wicked Malsum was so glad that he promised to give the Beaver whatever he might ask for. But when the beast asked for wings like a pigeon Malsum burst into mocking laughter and cried: "Ho, you with the tail like a file, what need have you of wings?" At this the Beaver became irate and, going to Glooskap,

The touch of an owl's feather or a flowering rush could kill Glooskap. Feather bonnets like this one of owl feathers were worn by many native peoples, for ceremony and to denote rank. (Pitt Rivers Museum, Oxford.)

Chief Bear Bull (opposite), of the Blackfeet, a tribe of the Algonquian linguistic group. (Illustration from Edward Curtis, *The North American Indian*, 1907–30.)

Malsum, the Wolf, and Glooskap were twins who between them made the world. Black American wolf by J. J. Audubon, from *The Viviparous Quadrupeds of North America*, 1846–54.

Moccasins were usually made of deer skin. (Illustration from H. R. Schoolcraft, *Narrative Journal of Travels from Detroit North-west through the Great Chain of American Lakes*, 1821.)

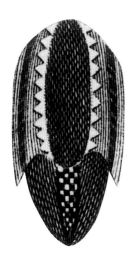

made a clean breast of what he had done. Glooskap, now thoroughly infuriated, dug up a fern-root and, rushing into the recesses of the forest, sought out his treacherous brother and with a blow of the fatal plant struck him dead.

When Glooskap had completed the world he made man and the smaller supernatural beings, such as fairies and dwarfs. He formed man from the trunk of an ash-tree, and the elves from its bark. He trained two birds to bring him the news of the world, but their absences were so prolonged that he selected a black and a white wolf as his attendants. He waged a strenuous and exterminating warfare on the evil monsters which then infested the world, and on the sorcerers and witches who were harmful to man. He levelled the hills and restrained the forces of nature in his mighty struggles, in which he towered to giant stature, his head and shoulders rising high above the clouds. Yet in his dealings with men he was gentle and quietly humorous, not to say ingenuous.

On one occasion he sought out a giant sorcerer named Win-pe, one of the most powerful of the evil influences then dwelling upon the earth. Win-pe shot upward till his head was above the tallest pine of the forest, but Glooskap, with a god-like laugh, grew till his head reached the stars, and tapped the wizard gently with the butt of his bow, so that he fell dead at his feet.

But although he exterminated many monsters and placed a check upon the advance of the forces of evil, Glooskap did not find that the race of men grew any better or wiser. In fact, the more he accomplished on their behalf, the worse they became, until at last they reached such a pitch of evil conduct that the god resolved to quit the world altogether. But with a feeling of consideration still for the beings he had created, he announced that within the next seven years he would grant to all and sundry any request they might make. A great many people were desirous of profiting by this offer, but it was with the utmost difficulty that they could discover Glooskap's whereabouts. Those who did find him and who chose injudiciously were severely punished, while those whose desires were reasonable were substantially rewarded.

Four Indians who reached Glooskap's abode found it a place of magical delights, a land fairer than the mind could conceive. Asked by the god what had brought them thither, one replied that his heart was evil and that anger had made him its slave, but that he wished to be meek and pious. The second, a poor man, desired to be rich, and the third, who was of low estate and despised by the folk of his tribe, wished to be universally honoured and respected. The fourth was a vain man, conscious of his good looks, whose appearance was eloquent of conceit. Although he was tall, he had stuffed fur into his moccasins to make him appear still taller, and his wish was that he might become bigger than any man of his tribe and that he might live for ages.

Glooskap drew four small boxes from his medicine-bag and gave one to each man, desiring that they should not open the boxes until they reached home. When the first three arrived at their respective lodges each opened his box, and found therein an unguent of great fragrance and richness, with which he rubbed himself. The wicked man became meek and patient, the poor man speedily grew wealthy, and the despised man became stately and respected. But the conceited man had stopped on his way home in a clearing in the woods, and, taking out his box, had anointed himself with the ointment it contained. His wish also was granted, but not exactly in the manner he expected, for he was changed into a pine-tree, the first of the species, and the tallest tree of the forest at that.

Glooskap and the Baby

Glooskap conquered the Kewawkqu', a race of giants and magicians, the Medecolin, who were cunning sorcerers, and Pamola, a wicked spirit of the night, besides many other fiends and felt great indeed. He boasted to a certain woman that there was nothing left for him to subdue.

Win-pe grew as tall as the tallest pine in the forest (above). Douglas fir and giant cedar. (Illustration from the Marquis of Lorne, *Canadian Pictures, c. 1884.*)

"Quah-beet, the Great Beaver, was hidden among the rushes" (left). Beaver pond trail, Algonquin Provincial Park, Ontario.

But the woman laughed and said: "Are you quite sure, Master? There is still one who remains unconquered, and nothing can overcome him."

In some surprise Glooskap inquired the name of this mighty individual.

"He is called Wasis," replied the woman; "but I strongly advise you to have no dealings with him."

Wasis was only the baby, who sat on the floor sucking a piece of maple-sugar and crooning a little song to himself. Now Glooskap had never married and was quite ignorant of how children were managed, but with perfect confidence he smiled at the baby and asked it to come to him. The baby smiled back at him, but never moved, whereupon Glooskap imitated the beautiful song of a certain bird. Wasis, however, paid no heed to him, but went on sucking his maple-sugar. Glooskap, unaccustomed to such treatment, lashed himself into furious rage, and in terrible and threatening accents ordered Wasis to come crawling to him at once. But Wasis burst into direful howling, which quite drowned the god's thunderous accents, and for all the threatenings of the deity he would not budge. Glooskap, now thoroughly aroused, brought all his magical resources to his aid. He recited the most terrible spells, the most dreadful incantations. He sang the songs which raised the dead, and which sent the devil scurrying to the nethermost depths of the pit. But Wasis evidently seemed to think this was all some sort of a game, for he merely smiled wearily and looked a trifle bored. At last Glooskap, in despair, rushed from the hut, while Wasis, sitting on the floor, cried, "Goo, goo," and crowed triumphantly. And to this day the Indians say that when a baby cries "Goo" he remembers the time when he conquered the mighty Glooskap.

"Wasis was only the baby". Chippeway woman and child. (Illustration from T. L. McKenney and J. Hall, *The Indian Tribes of North America*, 1846.)

How Glooskap Caught the Summer

A very beautiful myth tells how Glooskap captured the Summer. A long time ago Glooskap wandered very far north to the Ice-country, and, feeling tired and cold, sought shelter at a wigwam where dwelt a great giant—the giant Winter. Winter received the god hospitably, filled a pipe of tobacco for him, and entertained him with charming stories of the old time as he smoked. All the time, Winter was casting his spell over Glooskap, for as he talked drowsily and monotonously he gave forth a freezing atmosphere, so that Glooskap first dozed and then fell into a deep sleep—the heavy slumber of the winter season. For six whole months he slept, then the spell of the frost arose from his brain and he awoke. He took his way homeward and southward, and the farther south he fared the warmer it felt, and the flowers began to spring up out of the ground around his steps.

At length he came to a vast, trackless forest where, under primeval trees, many little people were dancing. The queen of these folk was Summer, a most exquisitely beautiful, if very tiny, creature. Glooskap caught the queen up in his great hand and, cutting a long lasso from the hide of a moose, secured it round her tiny frame. Then he ran away, letting the cord trail loosely behind him.

The tiny people, who were the Elves of Light, came clamouring shrilly after him, pulling frantically at the lasso. But as Glooskap ran, the cord ran out, and pull as they might they were left far behind.

Northward he journeyed once more, and came to the wigwam of Winter. The giant again received him hospitably, and began to tell the old stories whose vague charm had exercised such a fascination upon the god. But Glooskap, in his turn, began to speak. Summer was lying in his bosom, and her strength and heat sent forth such powerful magic that at length Winter began to show signs of distress. The sweat poured profusely down his face, and gradually he started to melt, as did his dwelling. Then slowly nature awoke, the song of birds was heard, first faintly, then more clearly and joyously. The thin green shoots of the young grass appeared, and the dead leaves of last autumn were carried down to the river by the melting snow. Lastly, the fairies came out, and Glooskap, leaving Summer with them, once more bent his steps southward.

Glooskap's Farewell

At length the day on which Glooskap was to leave the earth arrived, and to celebrate the event he caused a great feast to be made on the shores of Lake Minas. It was attended by all the animals, and when it drew to a close Glooskap entered his great canoe and slowly drifted out of sight. When they could see him no longer they still heard his beautiful singing growing fainter and fainter in the distance, until at last it died away altogether. Then a strange thing happened. The beasts, who up to this time had spoken but one language, could no longer understand each other, and in confusion fled away, never again to meet in friendly converse until Glooskap should return and revive the halcyon days of the Golden Age.

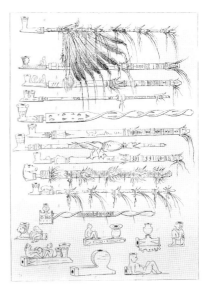

Winter filled a pipe of tobacco. Archaeological evidence suggests that tobacco-smoking in North America dates back 4,000 years or more. (Illustration from George Catlin, *Letters on the North American Indians*, 1841.)

Spearing fish in winter by Seth Eastman (1808–75). On frozen lakes and rivers, holes were cut in the ice for fishing. (U.S. Capitol Collection, Washington, D.C., North America.)

Buffalo hunt on snow shoes by George Catlin (1796–1872). A painter and traveller, Catlin spent many years among the tribes of the Plains and the Northwest. (*North American Indian Portfolio*, 1844.)

THE LORD OF COLD WEATHER

Chill breezes had long forewarned the geese of the coming cold season, and the constant cry from above of "honk, honk," told the Indians that the birds' migration was in progress.

The buffalo-hunters of the Blackfeet, an Algonquian tribe, were abroad with the object of procuring the thick robes and rich meat which would keep them warm and provide good fare through the desolate winter moons. Sacred Otter had been lucky. Many buffaloes had fallen to him, and he was busily occupied in skinning them. But while the braves plied their knives quickly and deftly, they did not heed the dun, lowering clouds heavy with tempest, hanging like a black curtain over the northern horizon. Suddenly the clouds swooped down from the heavens like a flight of black eagles, and with a roar, the blizzard was upon them.

Sacred Otter and his son crouched beneath the carcass of a dead buffalo for shelter. But the air was as chilled as water in which the ice is floating, and he knew that they would quickly perish unless they could find some better protection from the bitter wind. So he made a small *tepee*, or tent, out of the buffalo's hide, and both crawled inside. Against this makeshift shelter the snow quickly gathered and drifted, so that soon the inmates of the tiny lodge sank into a comfortable drowse induced by the gentle warmth. As Sacred Otter slept, he dreamed. Away in the distance he caught sight of a great *tepee*, crowned with a colour like the gold of sunlight, and painted with a cluster of stars symbolic of the North. The ruddy disc of the sun was pictured at the back, and to this was affixed the tail of the Sacred Buffalo. The skirts of the *tepee* were painted to represent ice, and on its side had been drawn four yellow legs with green claws, typical of the Thunder-bird. A buffalo in glaring red frowned above the door, and bunches of crow-feathers, with small bells attached, swung and tinkled in the breeze.

Sacred Otter, surprised at the unusual nature of the paintings, stood before the *tepee* lost in admiration of its decorations, when he was startled to hear a voice say:

"Who walks round my *tepee*? Come in—come in!"

Sacred Otter entered, and beheld a tall, white-haired man, clothed all in white, sitting at the back of the lodge. Sacred Otter took a seat, but the owner of the *tepee* never looked his way, smoking on in stolid silence. Before him was an earthen altar, on which was laid juniper, as in the Sun ceremonial. His face was painted yellow, with a red line in the region of the mouth, and another across the eyes to the ears. Across his breast he wore a mink-skin, and round his waist small strips of otter-skin, to all of which bells were attached. For a long time he kept silence, but at length he laid down his black stone pipe and addressed Sacred Otter as follows:

"I am Es-tonea-pesta, the Lord of Cold Weather and this, my dwelling, is the Snow-tepee, or Yellow Paint Lodge. I control and send the driving snow and biting winds from the Northland. You are here because I have taken pity upon you and on your son who was caught in the blizzard with you. Take this Snow-tepee with its symbols and medicines. Take also this mink-skin tobacco-pouch, this black stone pipe and my supernatural power. You must make a *tepee* similar to this on your return to camp."

The Lord of Cold Weather then minutely explained to Sacred Otter the symbols of which he must make use in painting the lodge, and gave him the songs and cermonial connected with it. At this juncture Sacred Otter awoke. He observed that the storm had abated somewhat, and as soon as

He wore a mink-skin and small strips of otter-skin. The wearing of particular fur indicated status. (Illustration by Karl Bodmer from M. A. P. Wied-Neuwied, *Voyage dans l'intérieur de l'Amérique du Nord*, 1840–43.)

"Sacred Otter had been lucky". Canada otter (left) by J. J. Audubon, from *The Viviparous Quadrupeds of North America*, 1846–54.

it grew fair enough, he and his son crawled from their shelter and tramped home waist-high through the soft snow. Sacred Otter spent the long, cold nights in making a model of the Snow-tepee and painting it as he had been directed in his dream. He also collected the plant medicines necessary for the ceremonial, and in the spring, when new lodges were made, he built and painted the Snow-tepee.

The power of Sacred Otter waxed great because of his possession of the Snow-lodge which the Lord of Cold had vouchsafed to him in his dream. This power was soon shown to be no mere dream. Once more, while hunting buffalo, Sacred Otter and several companions were caught in a blizzard when many a weary mile from camp. They appealed to Sacred Otter to utilize the medicine of the Lord of Cold Weather. Directing that several women and children who were with the party should be placed on sledges, and that the men should go in advance and break a passage through the snow for the horses, he took the mink tobacco-pouch and the black stone pipe he had received from the Cold-maker and commenced to smoke. He blew the smoke in the direction whence the storm came and prayed to the

Black stone pipe, Blackfeet or Cree, *c.* 1850. The black steatite from which the bowl is made is comparatively soft and easy to work when first mined.

Sacred Otter painted the model tepee (right). Piegan lodges were often painted, sometimes with incidents from the owner's career. (Illustration from Edward Curtis, *The North American Indian*, 1907–30.)

Indian encampment on Lake Huron by Paul Kane (1810–71). A Canadian painter, Kane was alerted to the plight of the Native Americans by George Catlin. (Royal Ontario Museum, Toronto.)

Lord of Cold Weather to have pity on the people. Gradually the storm-clouds broke and cleared and on every side blue sky was seen. The people hastened on, as they knew the blizzard was only being held back for a space. But their camp was at hand, and they soon reached it in safety.

Never again, however, would Sacred Otter use his mystic power. For he dreaded that he might offend the Lord of Cold Weather. And who could afford to do that?

CLOUD-CARRIER AND THE STAR-FOLK

A handsome youth once dwelt with his parents on the banks of Lake Huron. The old people were very proud of their boy, and intended that he should become a great warrior. When he grew old enough to prepare his medicine-bag he set off into the forest for that purpose. As he journeyed he grew weary, and lay down to sleep, and while he slept he heard a gentle voice whisper:

"Cloud-carrier, I have come to fetch you. Follow me."

The young man started to his feet.

"I am dreaming. It is but an illusion," he muttered to himself, as he gazed at the owner of the soft voice, who was a damsel of such marvellous beauty that the sleepy eyes of Cloud-carrier were quite dazzled.

"Follow me," she said again, and rose softly from the ground like this-tledown. To his surprise the youth rose along with her, as lightly and as easily. Higher they went, and still higher, far above the tree-tops and into the sky, till they passed at length through an opening in the spreading vault, and Cloud-carrier saw that he was in the country of the Star-people, and that his beautiful guide was no mortal maiden but a supernatural being. So fascinated was he by her sweetness and gentleness that he followed her till they came to a large lodge. Entering it at the invitation of the maiden, Cloud-carrier found it filled with weapons and ornaments of silver, worked in strange designs. For a time he wandered through the lodge, admiring and praising all he saw, his warrior-blood stirring at the sight of the rare weapons. Suddenly the lady cried:

"Hush! My brother approaches! Let me hide you. Quick!"

The young man crouched in a corner, and the damsel threw a richly coloured scarf over him. Scarcely had she done so when a grave and dignified warrior stalked into the lodge.

"Nemissa, my dear sister," he said, after a moment's pause, "have you not been forbidden to speak to the Earth-people? Perhaps you imagine you have hidden the young man, but you have not." Then, turning from the blushing Nemissa to Cloud-carrier, he added, good-naturedly:

"If you stay long there you will be very hungry. Come out and let us have a talk."

The youth did as he was bid, and the brother of Nemissa gave him a pipe and a bow and arrows. He gave him also Nemissa for his wife, and for a long time they lived together very happily.

Silver brooch dating from about 1850. Silverwork was introduced to the woodland tribes by Europeans who supplied both sheet silver and tools.

OTTER-HEART AND TEN PAIRS OF MOCCASINS

In the heart of a great forest lay a nameless little lake, and by its side dwelt two children. Wicked magicians had slain their parents while they were still of tender years, and the little orphans were obliged to fend for themselves. The younger of the two, a boy, learned to shoot with bow and arrow, and he soon acquired such skill that he rarely returned from a hunting expedition without a specimen of his prowess in the shape of a bird or a hare, which his elder sister would dress and cook.

When the boy grew older he naturally felt the need of some companionship other than that of his sister. During his long, solitary journeys in search of food he thought a good deal about the great world outside the barrier of the still, silent forest. He longed for the sound of human voices to replace the murmuring of the trees and the cries of the birds.

"Are there no Indians but ourselves in the whole world?" he would ask wistfully.

"I do not know," his sister invariably replied. Busying herself cheerfully about her household tasks, she knew nothing of the strange thoughts that were stirring in the mind of her brother.

But one day he returned from the chase in so discontented a mood that his unrest could no longer pass unnoticed. In response to solicitous inquiries from his sister, he said abruptly:

"Make me ten pairs of moccasins. Tomorrow I am going to travel into the great world."

The girl was much disturbed by this communication, but like a good Indian maiden, she did as he requested her and kept a respectful silence.

Early on the following morning the youth, whose name was Otter-heart, set out on his quest. He soon came to a clearing in the forest, but to his disappointment he found that the tree-stumps were old and rotten.

"It is a long, long time", he said mournfully, "since there were Indians living in this place."

In order that he might find his way back, he suspended a pair of moccasins from the branch of a tree, and continued his journey. Other clearings he reached in due time, each showing traces of a more recent occupation than the last, but still it seemed to him that a long time must have elapsed since the trees were cut down, so he hung up a pair of moccasins at each stage of his journey, and pursued his course in search of human beings.

At last he saw before him an Indian village, which he approached with mingled feelings of pleasure and trepidation, natural enough in one who, since his early childhood, had spoken to no one but his sister.

Micmac moccasins. The Micmacs of the northeast forests made elaborately beaded garments for special occasions. (Pitt Rivers Museum, Oxford.)

The brother of Nemissa gave him a pipe. (Illustration from H. R. Schoolcraft, *Narrative Journal of Travels from Detroit North-west through the Great Chain of American Lakes*, 1821.)

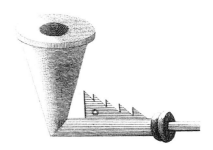

Good and Wicked Wives

On the outskirts of the village some youths of about his own age were engaged in a game of ball, in which they courteously invited the stranger to join. Very soon he had forgotten his natural shyness so far as to enter into the sport with whole-hearted zest and enjoyment. His new companions, for their part, were filled with astonishment at his skill and agility, and, wishing to do him honour, led him to the great lodge and introduced him to their chief.

Now the chief had two daughters, one of whom was surnamed "The Good" and the other "The Wicked." To the guest the names sounded rather meaningful, and he was not a little embarrassed when the chief begged him to marry the maidens.

"I will marry The Good," he declared.

But the chief would not agree to that.

"You must marry both," he said firmly.

Here was a dilemma for our hero, who had no wish to wed the cross,

A game of ball. Ball-games such as lacrosse were sometimes played by teams with several hundred players on each side. (Illustration from George Catlin, *North American Portfolio*, 1844.)

ugly sister. He tried hard to think of a way to escape this fate.

"I am going to visit So-and-so," he said at last, mentioning the name of one of his companions at ball, and he dressed himself carefully as though he were about to pay a ceremonious visit.

Directly he was out of sight of the chief's lodge, however, he took to his heels and ran into the forest as hard as he could. Meanwhile the maidens sat waiting for their intended bridegroom. When some hours passed without there being any sign of his coming they became alarmed, and set off to look for him.

Toward nightfall the young Otter-heart relaxed his speed. "I am quite safe now," he thought. He did not know that the sisters had the resources of magic at their command. Suddenly he heard wild laughter behind him. Recognizing the shrill voice of The Wicked, he knew that he was discovered, and cast about for a refuge. The only likely place was in the branches of a dense fir-tree, and almost as soon as the thought entered his mind he was at the top. His satisfaction was short-lived. In a moment the laughter of the women broke out anew, and they commenced to hew down the tree. But Otter-heart himself was not without some acquaintance with magic art. Plucking a small fir-cone from the the tree-top, he threw it into the air, jumped astride it and rode down the wind for half a mile or more. The sisters, absorbed in their task of cutting down the tree, did not notice that their bird had flown. When at last the great fir crashed to the ground and the youth was nowhere to be seen, the pursuers tore their hair in rage and disappointment.

The Magic Lodges

Only on the following evening did they overtake Otter-heart again. This time he had entered a hollow cedar-tree, the hard wood of which he thought would defy their axes. But he had under-estimated the energy of the sisters. In a short time the tree showed the effect of their blows, and Otter-heart called on his guardian spirit to break one of the axes.

His wish was promptly granted, but the other sister continued her labours with increased energy. Otter-heart now wished that the other axe might break, and again his desire was fulfilled. The sisters were at a loss to know what to do.

"We cannot take him by force," said one; "we must take him by subtlety. Let each do her best, and the one who gets him can keep him."

So they departed, and Otter-heart was free to emerge from his prison. He travelled another day's journey from the spot, and at last, reaching a place where he thought he would be safe, he laid down his blanket and went in search of food. Fortune favoured the hunter, and he shortly returned with a fine beaver. What was his amazement when he beheld a handsome lodge where he had left his blanket!

"It must be those women again," he muttered, preparing to fly. But the light shone so warmly from the lodge, and he was so tired and hungry, that he conquered his fears and entered. Within he found a tall, thin woman, pale and hungry-eyed, but rather pretty. Taking the beaver, she proceeded to cook it. As she did so Otter-heart noticed that she ate all the best parts herself, and when the meal was set out only the poorest pieces remained for him. This was so unlike an Indian housewife that he cast reproaches at her and accused her of greediness. As he spoke a curious change came over her. Her features grew longer and thinner. In a moment she had turned into a wolf and slunk into the forest. It was The Wicked, who had made herself pretty by means of magic, but could not conceal her voracious nature.

Otter-heart was glad to have found her out. He journeyed on still farther, laid down his blanket, and went to look for game. This time several beavers rewarded his skill, and he carried them to the place where he had left his blanket. Another handsome lodge had been erected there! More than ever he wanted to run away, but once more his hunger and fatigue detained him.

"Perhaps it is The Good," he said. "I shall go inside, and if she has laid my blanket near her couch I shall take it for a sign and she shall become my wife."

He entered the lodge, and found a small, pretty woman busily engaged in household duties. Sure enough, she had laid his blanket near her couch. She examined the beavers, then prepared and cooked them, giving the finest morsels to her new husband, who was thoroughly pleased with his wife.

Hearing a sound in the night, Otter-heart awoke, and fancied he saw his wife chewing birch-bark. When he told her of the dream in the morning she did not laugh, but looked very serious.

"Tell me," asked Otterheart, "why did you examine the beavers so closely yesterday?"

Otter-heart travelled another day's journey. In dense woodland, travel by water was most efficient. (Rev E. R. Young, *By Canoe and Dog Train among the Cree and Salteaux Indians*, 1903.)

Birch-bark container in the shape of a canoe and decorated by scraping away the dark outer layer to create patterns *c.* 1860, Chippewa or Ojibwa.

"They were my relatives," she replied; "the beavers cooked were my cousin, my aunt, and my great-uncle."

Otter-heart was more than ever delighted, for the otters, his totem-kin and the beavers had always been on very good terms. He promised never to kill any more beavers, but only deer and birds, and he and his wife, The Good, lived very happily together for a long time.

THE DEATH-SWING

An Ojibway, or Chippeway, hunter was greatly devoted to his wife. As a proof of his affection, he always presented her with the most delicate morsels from the game he killed. This aroused the jealousy and envy of his mother, who lived with them, and who imagined that these little attentions should be paid to her and not to the younger woman. The latter, quite unaware of her mother-in-law's attitude, cooked and ate the gifts her husband brought her. Being a woman of a gentle and agreeable disposition, who spent most of her time attending to her household duties and watching over her child and a little orphan boy whom she had adopted, she tried to make friends with the old dame, and was grieved and disappointed when the latter would not respond to her advances.

The mother-in-law nursed her grievance until it seemed of gigantic proportions. Her heart grew blacker and blacker against her son's wife, and at last she determined to kill her. For a time she could think of no way to put her evil intention into action, but finally she hit upon a plan.

One day she disappeared from the lodge, and returned after a space looking very happy and good-tempered. The younger woman was surprised and delighted at the alteration. This was an agreeably different person from the nagging, cross-grained old creature who had made her life a burden! The old woman repeatedly absented herself from her home after this, returning on each occasion with a pleased and contented smile on her wrinkled face. By and by the wife allowed her curiosity to get the better of her and she asked the meaning of her mother-in-law's happiness.

"If you must know", replied the old woman, "I have made a beautiful swing down by the lake, and always when I swing on it I feel so well and happy that I cannot help smiling."

The young woman begged that she too might be allowed to enjoy the swing.

"To-morrow you may accompany me," was the reply. But next day the old woman had some excuse, and so on, day after day, till the curiosity of her son's wife was very keen. Thus when the elder woman said one day, "Come with me, and I will take you to the swing. Tie up your baby and leave him in charge of the orphan," the other complied eagerly, and was ready in a moment to go with her mother-in-law.

When they reached the shores of the lake they found a lithe sapling which hung over the water.

"Here is my swing," said the old creature, and she cast aside her robe, fastened a thong to her waist and to the sapling, and swung far out over the lake. She laughed so much and seemed to find the pastime so pleasant

An Apache babe (opposite). Cradleboards and baskets were used to carry swaddled babies throughout the continent. This one is from the Southwest. (Illustration from Edward Curtis, *The North American Indian*, 1907–30.)

The Thousand Islands (right), where the St Lawrence River leaves Lake Ontario. (Illustration from the Marquis of Lorne, *Canadian Pictures*, c. 1884.)

A Cheyenne woman's dress of deerskin, decorated with beads and shells, c. 1870. The Cheyenne moved from the eastern woodlands to the northern prairies in about 1700.

Mother-in-law cut the thong. (Illustration by Karl Bodmer from M. A. P. Wied-Neuwied, *Voyage dans l'intérieur de l'Amérique du Nord,* 1840–43.)

that her daughter-in-law was more anxious than ever to try it for herself and asked the other if she might have a turn.

"Let me tie the thong for you," said the old woman, when she had tired of swinging. Her companion threw off her robe and allowed the leather thong to be fastened round her waist. When all was ready she was commanded to swing. Out over the water she went fearlessly, but as she did so the jealous old mother-in-law cut the thong, and she fell into the lake.

The old creature, exulting over the success of her cruel scheme, dressed herself in her victim's clothes and returned to the lodge. But the baby cried and refused to be fed by her, and the orphan boy cried too, for the young woman had been almost a mother to him since his parents had died.

"Where is the baby's mother?" the orphan asked, when some hours had passed and she did not return.

"At the swing," replied the old woman, roughly.

When the hunter returned from the chase he brought with him, as usual, some morsels of game for his wife, and, never dreaming that the woman bending over the child might not be she, he gave them to her. The lodge was dark, for it was evening, and his mother wore the clothes of his wife and imitated her voice and movements, so that his error was not surprising. Greedily the old woman seized the tender pieces of meat, which she cooked and ate herself.

The heart of the little orphan was so sore that he could not sleep. In the middle of the night he rose and went to look for his foster-mother. Down by the lake he found the swing with the thong cut, and he knew that she had been killed. Crying bitterly, he crept home to his couch, and in the morning told the hunter all that he had seen.

"Say nothing," said the chief, "but come with me to hunt, and in the evening return to the shores of the lake with the child, while I pray to Manitou that he may send me back my wife."

So they went off in search of game without a word to the old woman; nor did they stay to eat, but set out directly it was light. At sunset they made their way to the lake-side, the little orphan carrying the baby. Here the hunter blackened his face and prayed earnestly that the Great Manitou might send back his wife. While he prayed the orphan amused the child by singing quaint little songs, but at last the baby grew weary and hungry and began to cry.

Far in the lake his mother heard the sound, and skimmed over the water in the shape of a great white gull. When she touched the shore she became a woman again, and hugged the child to her heart's content. The orphan boy besought her to return to them.

"Alas!" said she, "I have fallen into the hands of the Water Manitou, and he has wound his silver tail about me, so that I never can escape."

As she spoke, the little lad saw that her waist was encircled by a band of gleaming silver, one end of which was in the water. At length she declared that it was time for her to return to the home of the water-god, and after having exacted a promise from the boy that he would bring her baby there every day, she became a gull again and flew away. The hunter was informed of all that had passed, and straightway determined that he would be present on the following evening. All next day he fasted and besought the good-will of Manitou, and when the night began to fall he hid himself on the shore till his wife appeared. Hastily emerging from his concealment, the hunter poised her spear and struck the girdle with all his force. The silver band parted, and the woman was free to return home with her husband.

Overjoyed at her restoration, he led her gently to the lodge, where his mother was sitting by the fire. At the sight of her daughter-in-law, whom she thought she had drowned in the lake, she started up in such fear and astonishment that she tripped, overbalanced, and fell into the fire. Before they could pull her out the flames had risen to the smoke-hole, and when the fire died down no woman was there, but a great black bird, which rose slowly from the smoking embers and flew out of the lodge. After this it was never seen again.

As for the others, they lived long and happily, undisturbed by the jealousy and hatred of the malicious crone.

HOW MAIZE WAS GIVEN TO THE INDIANS

A lad of fourteen or fifteen dwelt with his parents, brothers and sisters in a beautifully situated little lodge. The family, though poor, were very happy and contented. The father was a hunter who was not lacking in courage and skill, but there were times when he could scarcely supply the wants of his family, and as none of his children was old enough to help him, things went badly with them. The lad was of a cheerful and contented disposition, like his father, and his great desire was to benefit his people. The time had come for him to observe the initial fast prescribed for all Indian boys of his age, and his mother made him a little fasting-lodge in a remote spot where he might not suffer interruption during his ordeal.

Skeleton of a Chippewa lodge. The domed framework of ironwood or elm would be covered with bark and matting. (Illustration from T. L. McKenney *Sketches of a Tour of the Lakes*, 1827.)

Belt of silver and turquoise conches, c. 1890. Although typical of the Navajo of New Mexico, this type of belt was widely traded to tribes in other parts of North America.

Feathered warbonnet (above), probably Lakota. This backview shows some thirty golden eagle feathers attached to a buckskin cap covered with ermine skins.

A youth richly dressed. Garments of woodland warriors worked in moosehair embroidery on birch bark, probably by Chippewa or Huron Indians.

Indian village of Secotan (opposite), by John White, 1585. White made several detailed drawings at Secotan. This one clearly shows the fields of maize, marked "corne", growing by the village. (British Museum.)

Thither the boy hastened, meditating on the goodness of the Great Spirit, who had made all things beautiful in the fields and forests for the enjoyment of man. The desire to help his fellows was strong within him, and he prayed that some means to that end might be revealed to him in a dream. On the third day of his fast he was too weak to ramble through the forest, and as he lay in a state between sleeping and waking there came towards him a beautiful youth, richly dressed in green robes, and wearing on his head wonderful green plumes.

"The Great Spirit has heard your prayers," said the youth, and his voice was like the sound of the wind sighing through the grass. "Hearken to me and you shall have your desire fulfilled. Arise and wrestle with me."

The lad obeyed. Though his limbs were weak his brain was clear and active, and he felt he must obey the stranger. After a long, silent struggle the latter said: "That will do for to-day. Tomorrow I shall come again."

The lad lay back exhausted, but on the morrow the green-clad stranger reappeared, and the conflict was renewed. As the struggle went on the youth felt himself grow stronger and more confident, and before leaving him for the second time the supernatural visitor offered him some words of praise and encouragement.

On the third day the youth, pale and feeble, was again summoned to the contest. As he grasped his opponent the very contact seemed to give him new strength, and he fought more and more bravely, till his lithe companion was forced to cry out that he had had enough. Ere he took his departure the visitor told the lad that the following day would put an end to his trials.

"To-morrow", said he, "your father will bring you food, and that will help you. In the evening I shall come and wrestle with you. I know that you are destined to succeed and to obtain your heart's desire. When you have thrown me, strip off my garments and plumes, bury me where I fall, and keep the earth above me moist and clean. Once a month let my remains be covered with fresh earth, and you shall see me again, clothed in my green garments and plumes." So saying, he vanished.

Next day the lad's father brought him food; the youth, however, begged that it might be set aside till evening. Once again the stranger appeared. Though he had eaten nothing, the hero's strength, as before, seemed to increase as he struggled, and at length he threw his opponent. Then he stripped off his garments and plumes, and buried him in the earth, not without sorrow in his heart for the slaying of such a beautiful youth. His task done, he returned to his parents, and soon recovered his strength. But he never forgot the grave of his friend. Not a weed was allowed to grow on it, and finally he was rewarded by seeing the green plumes rise above the earth and broaden out into graceful leaves. When the autumn came he requested his father to accompany him to the place. By this time the plant was at its full height, tall and beautiful, with golden tassels. The elder man was filled with surprise and admiration.

"It is my friend," murmured the youth, "the friend of my dreams."

"It is Mon-da-min," said his father, "the spirit's grain, the gift of the Great Spirit."

And in this manner was maize given to the Indians.

Their rype corne.

Their greene corne.

Corne newly sprong.

Their sitting at meate.

The place of solemne prayer.

The house wherin the Tombe of their Herounds standeth.

SECOTON.

A Ceremony in their prayers wth strange iestures and songes dansing abowt posts carued on the topps lyke mens faces.

The elder daughter married a grizzly bear.
Grizzly bear by J. J. Audubon, from *The
Viviparous Quadrupeds of North
America*, 1846–54.

BEARSKIN-WOMAN

Once there dwelt together nine children, seven boys and two girls. While the six older brothers were away on the war-path the elder daughter, whose name was Bearskin-woman, married a grizzly bear. Her father was so enraged that he collected his friends and ordered them to surround the grizzly's cave and slay him. When the girl heard that her spouse had been killed, she took a piece of his skin and wore it as an amulet. Through the agency of her husband's supernatural power, one dark night she was changed into a grizzly bear, and rushed through the camp, killing all the people, even her own father and mother, sparing only her youngest brother and her sister, Okinai and Sinopa. She then took her former shape and returned to the lodge occupied by the two orphans, who were greatly terrified when they heard her muttering to herself, planning their deaths.

Sinopa had gone to the river one day, when she met her six brothers returning from the war-path. She told them what had happened in their absence. They reassured her and bade her gather a large number of prickly pears. These she was to strew in front of the lodge, leaving only a small path uncovered by them. In the dead of night Okinai and Sinopa crept out of the lodge, picking their way down the little path that was free from the prickly pears, and meeting their six brothers, who were awaiting them. The Bearskin-woman heard them leaving the lodge, and rushed out into the open, only to tread on the prickly pears. Roaring with pain and anger, she immediately assumed her bear shape and rushed furiously at her brothers. But Okinai rose to the occasion. He shot an arrow into the air, and as far as it flew the brothers and sister found themselves just that distance in front of the savage animal behind them.

The beast gained on them, however, but Okinai waved a magic feather, and thick underbrush rose in its path. Again Bearskin-woman made headway. Okinai caused a lake to spring up before her. Yet again she neared the brothers and sister, and this time Okinai raised a great tree, into which the refugees climbed. The Grizzly-woman, however, succeeded in dragging four of the brothers from the tree, when Okinai shot an arrow into the air. Immediately his little sister sailed into the sky. Six times more he shot an arrow, and each time a brother went up, Okinai himself following them as the last arrow soared into the blue. Thus the orphans became stars, and one can see that they took the same position in the sky as they had occupied in the tree, for the small star at one side of the bunch is Sinopa, while the four who huddle together at the bottom are those who had been dragged from the branches by Bearskin-woman.

THE BEAVER MEDICINE LEGEND

Two brothers dwelt together in the old time. The elder, who was named Nopatsis, was married to a woman who was wholly evil, and who hated his younger brother, Akaiyan. Daily the wife pestered her husband to be rid of Akaiyan, but he would not agree to part with his only brother, for they had been together through long years of hardship—indeed, since their parents had left them together as little helpless orphans—and they were everything to each other. So the wife of Nopatsis resorted to a ruse well known to women whose hearts are evil. One day when her husband returned from the chase, he found her lamenting with torn clothes and disordered appearance. She told him that Akaiyan had treated her brutally. The lie entered into the heart of Nopatsis and made it heavy, so that in time he conceived a hatred of his innocent brother, and debated with himself how he should rid himself of Akaiyan.

Summer arrived, and with it the moulting season, when the wild waterfowl shed their feathers, with which the Indians fitted their arrows. Near Nopatsis's lodge there was a great lake, to which these birds resorted in large numbers, and to this place the brothers went to collect feathers with which to plume their darts. They built a raft to enable them to reach an island in the middle of the lake, making it of logs bound securely with buffalo-hide. Embarking, they sailed to the little island and walked along its shores, looking for suitable feathers. They parted in the quest, and after some time Akaiyan, who had wandered far along the strand, suddenly looked up to see his brother on the raft sailing toward the mainland. He called loudly to him to return, but Nopatsis replied that he deserved to perish there because of the brutal manner in which he had treated his sister-in-law. Akaiyan solemnly swore that he had not injured her in any way, but Nopatsis only jeered at him and rowed away. Soon he was lost to sight, and Akaiyan sat down and wept bitterly. He prayed earnestly to the nature spirits and to the sun and moon, after

He shot an arrow into the air. Feathered arrow by Karl Bodmer from M. A. P. Wied-Neuwied, *Voyage dans l'intérieur de l'Amérique du Nord*, 1840–43.

which he felt greatly uplifted. Then he improvised a shelter of branches, and made a bed of feathers of the most comfortable description. He lived well on the ducks and geese which frequented the island, and made a warm robe against the winter season from their skins. He was careful also to preserve many of the tame birds for his winter food.

One day he encountered the lodge of a beaver, and while he looked at it curiously, he became aware of the presence of one of the little animals.

"My father desires that you will enter his dwelling," said the beaver. So Akaiyan accepted the invitation and entered the lodge, where the Great Beaver, attended by his wife and family, received him. He was, indeed, the chief of all the beavers, and white with the snows of countless winters. Akaiyan told the Beaver how cruelly he had been treated, and the wise animal sympathized with him and invited him to spend the winter in his lodge, when he would learn many wonderful and useful things. Akaiyan gratefully accepted the invitation, and when the beavers closed up their lodge for the winter he remained with them. They kept him warm by placing their thick, soft tails on his body, and taught him the secret of the healing arts, the use of tobacco and various ceremonial dances, songs and prayers belonging to the great mystery of medicine.

The summer returned, and on parting, the Beaver asked Akaiyan to choose a gift. He chose the Beaver's youngest child, with whom he had contracted a strong friendship, but the father prized his little one greatly, and would not at first permit him to go. At length, however, Great Beaver gave way to Akaiyan's entreaties and allowed him to take Little Beaver with him, counselling him to construct a sacred Beaver Bundle when the two of them arrived at his native village.

In due time Nopatsis came to the island on his raft, and, wishing to

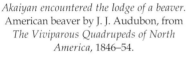

Akaiyan encountered the lodge of a beaver.
American beaver by J. J. Audubon, from *The Viviparous Quadrupeds of North America*, 1846–54.

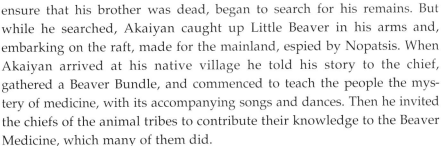

Indians as Beaver and Snake. Symbolic body painting was often practised by members of societies within tribes. (Illustration from George Catlin, *O-Kee-pa: A Religious Ceremony*, 1867.)

A beaver village may consist of several lodges, each up to 7 metres in diameter, with a camouflaged underwater entrance. (Illustration from the Marquis of Lorne, *Canadian Pictures*, c. 1884.)

ensure that his brother was dead, began to search for his remains. But while he searched, Akaiyan caught up Little Beaver in his arms and, embarking on the raft, made for the mainland, espied by Nopatsis. When Akaiyan arrived at his native village he told his story to the chief, gathered a Beaver Bundle, and commenced to teach the people the mystery of medicine, with its accompanying songs and dances. Then he invited the chiefs of the animal tribes to contribute their knowledge to the Beaver Medicine, which many of them did.

Having accomplished his task of instruction, which occupied him all the winter, Akaiyan returned to the island with Little Beaver, who had been of immense service to him in teaching the Indians the medicine songs and dances. He returned Little Beaver to his parents, and received in exchange for him a sacred pipe, being also instructed in its accompanying songs and ceremonial dances. On the island he found the bones of his credulous and vengeful brother, who had met with the fate he had purposed for the innocent Akaiyan. Every spring Akaiyan visited the beavers, and as regularly he received something to add to the Beaver Medicine Bundle, until it reached the great size it now has. And he married and founded a race of medicine-men who have handed down the traditions and ceremonials of the Beaver Medicine to the present day.

THE SOCIETY OF YOUNG DOGS

One day a young brave of the Cree tribe had gone out from his village to catch eagles, in order to provide himself with feathers for a war-bonnet and to tie in his hair. Now the Crees caught eagles in this fashion: on the top of a hill frequented by these birds they would dig a pit and cover it over with a roof of poles, cunningly concealing the structure with grass. A piece of meat was fastened to the poles, so that the eagles could not carry it off. Then the Indian, taking off his clothes, would descend into the pit and remain there for hours, or days as the case might be, until an eagle was attracted by the bait, when he would put his hand between the poles, seize the bird by the feet and quickly dispatch it.

The young brave whose fortune it was to discover the Young Dog Dance had prepared the trap in this way, and was lying in the pit, praying that an eagle might come and bring his uncomfortable vigil to an end. Suddenly he heard a sound of drumming, distant but quite distinct, though he could not tell from what direction it proceeded. All night the mysterious noise continued. Next night as he lay in the same position he heard it again, and resolved to find out its origin, so he clambered out of his pit and went off in the direction from which the drum-beating seemed to proceed. At last, when dawn was near, he reached the shores of a great lake. Here he stopped, for the sounds quite evidently came from the lake. All that day he sat by the water bemoaning his ill-luck and praying for better fortune. When night fell the drumming began anew, and the young man saw countless animals and birds swimming in the lake. He remained on the lake-shore for four days, till at length, worn out by fatigue and hunger (for

War bonnet (Illustration by Karl Bodmer from M. A. P. Wied-Neuwied, *Voyage dans l'intérieur de l'Amérique du Nord*, 1840–43.)

The Buffalo bull gave his strength and endurance. American bison or buffalo (right) by J. J. Audubon, from *The Viviparous Quadrupeds of North America*, 1846–54.

many days had elapsed since he had last eaten), he fell asleep.

When he awoke he found himself in a large lodge, surrounded by many people, some of whom were dancing, while others sat round the walls. All these people wore robes made from the skins of various animals or birds. They were, in fact, the animals the Young Indian had seen swimming in the water, who had changed themselves into human shape. A chief at the back of the lodge stood up and addressed him thus:

"My friend, we have heard your prayers, and our desire is to help you. You see these people? They represent the animals. I am the Dog. The Great Spirit is very fond of dogs. I have much power, and my power I shall give to you, so that you may be like me, and my spirit will always protect you. Take this dance home to your people, and it will make them lucky in war." And he imparted the nature of the rite to the Indian by action.

The Dog turned from the Cree brave and his eye swept the company.

"Brothers", he said, "I have given him my power. Will you not pity him and give him the power you have?"

For a time there was silence. No one seemed disposed to respond to the chief's appeal. At last the Owl rose.

"I will help you," he said to the young man. "I have power to see in the dark wherever I may go. When you go out at night I will be near you, and you shall see as well as I do. Take these feathers and tie them in your hair." And, giving him a bunch of feathers, the Owl sat down.

There was a pause, and the next to rise was the Buffalo Bull, who gave to the young Indian his strength and endurance and the power to trample his enemies underfoot. As a token he gave him a shoulder-belt of tanned buffalo-hide, bidding him wear it when he went on the war-path.

By and by the Porcupine stood up and addressed the guest. Giving him some of his quills with which to ornament the leather belt, he said:

"I also will help you. I can make my enemies as weak as women, so that they fly before me. When you fight your foes shall flee and you shall overcome them."

Another long silence ensued, and when at last the Eagle rose every one listened to hear what he had to say.

"I also", he said majestically, "will be with you wherever you go, and will give you my prowess in war, so that you may kill your foes as I do." As he spoke he handed to the brave some eagle feathers for the man to tie in his hair.

The Whooping Crane followed, and gave him a bone from its wing for a war-whistle to frighten his enemies away.

The Deer and the Bear came next, the one giving him swiftness, with a rattle as token, and the other hardiness, and a strip of fur for his belt.

After he had received these gifts from the animals the brave lay down and fell asleep again. When he awoke he found himself on the shores of the lake once more.

Returning home, he taught the Crees the Young Dog Dance, which was to make them skilful in war, and showed them the articles he had received from the Owl, the Buffalo, the Porcupine, the Eagle, the Crane, the Deer and the Bear. So the young men formed a Society of Young Dogs, which continued to practise the dance and obtain the benefits.

"Robes made from the skins of various animals or birds". (Illustration from the Marquis of Lorne, Canadian Pictures, c. 1884.)

The Blackfeet were moving camp. The horse gave Indians much greater mobility and ease of transport. (Illustration from the Marquis of Lorne, *Canadian Pictures, c.* 1884.)

A Crow village (below). Meat is being dried for pemmican. (Illustration from George Catlin, *Letters on the North American Indians,* 1841.)

THE FRIENDLY WOLF

On one occasion when the Blackfeet were moving camp, they were attacked by a number of Crow Indians who had been lying in wait for them. The Blackfeet were travelling slowly in a long, straggling line, with the old men and the women and children in the middle, and a band of warriors in front and in the rear. The Crows made an ambush for their enemies and rushed out on the middle portion of the line. Before either party of the Blackfeet warriors could reach the scene of the struggle many of the women and children had perished, and others were taken captive by the attacking force.

Among the prisoners was a young woman called Sits-by-the-door. Many weary miles lay between them and the Crow camp on the Yellowstone River, but at length the tired captives, mounted with their captors on jaded horses, arrived at their destination. The warrior who had taken Sits-by-the-door prisoner now presented her to a friend of his, who in turn gave her into the keeping of his wife, who was somewhat older than her charge. The young Blackfeet woman was cruelly treated by the Crow into whose possession she had passed. Every night he tied her feet together so that she might not escape, and also tied a rope round her waist, the other end of which he fastened to his wife. The Crow woman, however, was not unmoved by the wretchedness of her prisoner. While her husband was out she managed to converse with her and to show her that she pitied her misfortunes. One day she informed Sits-by-the-door that she had over-heard her husband and his companions plotting to kill her, but she added that when darkness fell she would help her to escape. When night came the Crow woman waited until the deep breathing of her husband told her that he was sound asleep; then, rising cautiously, she loosened the ropes that bound her captive, and, giving her a pair of moccasins, a flint and a small sack of pemmican, bade her make haste and escape from the fate that would surely befall her if she remained where she was. The trembling woman obeyed, and travelled at a good pace all night. At dawn she hid in the dense undergrowth, hoping to escape observation should her captors pursue her. They, meanwhile, had discovered her absence, and were searching high and low, but no tracks were visible, and at last, wearied with their unprofitable search, they gave up the chase and returned to their homes.

When the woman had journeyed on for four nights she stopped concealing herself in the daytime and travelled straight on. She was not yet out of danger, however, for her supply of pemmican was soon exhausted, and she found herself face to face with the miseries of starvation. Her moccasins, besides, were worn to holes and her feet were cut and bleeding, while, to add to her misfortunes, a huge wolf dogged her every movement. In vain she tried to run away; her strength was exhausted and she sank to the ground. Nearer and nearer came the great wolf, and at last he lay down at her feet. Whenever the woman walked on her way the wolf followed, and when she lay down to rest he lay down also.

At length she begged her strange companion to help her, for she knew that unless she obtained food very soon she must die. The animal trotted away, and returned shortly with a buffalo calf which it had killed, and laid it at the woman's feet. With the aid of the flint—one of the gifts with which the Crow woman had sped her unhappy guest—she built a fire and cooked some of the buffalo meat. Thus refreshed, she proceeded on her way. Again and again the wolf provided food in a similar manner, until at length they reached the Blackfeet camp. The woman led the animal into her lodge and related to her friends all that had befallen her in the Crow camp, and the manner of her escape. She also told them how the wolf had befriended her, and begged them to treat it kindly. But soon

"A huge wolf dogged her every movement". Red wolf by J. J. Audubon, from *The Viviparous Quadrupeds of North America*, 1846–54.

The Yellowstone River (left) ran through the territories inhabited by both Blackfeet and Crow. Though neighbours, the two tribes belonged to different linguistic groups.

Blackfeet country. Traditionally the Blackfeet ranged the prairies along the Bow River. (Illustration from Edward Curtis, *The North American Indian*, 1907–30.)

afterward she fell ill, and the poor wolf was driven out of the village by the Indian dogs. Every evening he would come to the top of a hill overlooking the camp and watch the lodge where Sits-by-the-door dwelt. Though he was still fed by her friends, after a time he disappeared and was seen no more.

THE STORY OF SCAR-FACE

Scar-face was brave but poor. His parents had died while he was still a boy, and he had no near relations. But his heart was high, and he was a mighty hunter. The old men said that Scar-face had a future before him, but the young braves teased him because of a mark across his face, left by the rending claw of a great grizzly bear which he had killed during the course of a close fight.

The chief of his tribe possessed a beautiful daughter, whom all the young men desired in marriage. Scar-face also had fallen in love with her, but he felt ashamed to declare his passion because of his poverty. The maiden had already repulsed half the braves of his tribe. Why, he argued should she accept him, poor and disfigured as he was?

One day he passed her as she sat outside her lodge. He cast a penetrating glance at her—a glance which was observed by one of her previously unsuccessful suitors. This man sneeringly remarked: "Scar-face would marry our chief's daughter! She does not desire a man without a blemish. Ha, Scar-face, now is your chance!"

Scar-face turned upon the jeerer, and in his quiet yet dignified manner remarked that it was indeed his intention to ask the chief's daughter to be his wife. His announcement met with ridicule, but he took no notice of it and sought out the girl.

He found her by the river, pulling rushes to make baskets. Approaching, he respectfully addressed her.

"I am poor," he said, "but my heart is rich in love for you. I have no wealth of furs or pemmican. I live by my bow and spear. I love you. Will you dwell with me in my lodge and be my wife?"

The Sun-God's Decree

The girl regarded him with bright, shy eyes peering up through lashes as the morning sun peers through the branches.

"My husband would not be poor," she faltered, "for my father, the chief, is wealthy and has abundance in his lodge. But it has been laid upon me by the Sun-god that I may not marry."

"These are heavy words," said Scar-face sadly. "Is there no way in which that decision can be changed?"

"On one condition only," replied the girl. "Seek the Sun-god and ask him to release me from my promise. If he consents to do so, request him to remove the scar from your face as a sign that I may know that he has agreed and will give me to you."

Baskets have been made for storage, transport and cookery from every kind of natural material, from rushes to bark. (Illustration from Smithsonian, *Report of the National Museum*, 1864.)

"Scar-face sought the home of the Sun-god" (left). This area of the Glacier National Park in Montana is known as "Going-to-the-Sun-Road".

A sun symbol painted on a buckskin robe, probably Sioux, *c.* 1870. Circular sun symbols are found in paintings, petroglyphs and in the shape of buildings throughout North America.

Morning Star symbol worked in blue beads on a horsehead ornament by the Crow Indians of the Central Plains as a sign of protection.

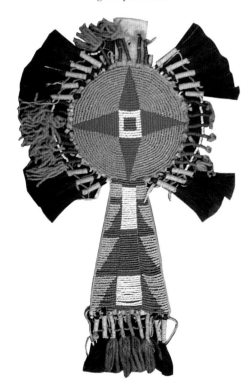

Scar-face was sad at heart, for he could not believe that the Sun-god, having chosen such a beautiful maiden for himself, would renounce her. But he gave the chief's daughter his promise that he would seek out the god in his own bright country and ask him to grant his request.

For many moons Scar-face sought the home of the Sun-god. He traversed wide plains and dense forests, crossed rivers and lofty mountains, yet never the least trace of the golden gates of the dwelling of the God of Light could he see.

Many inquiries did he make from the wild creatures of the forest—the wolf, the bear, the badger. But none knew the way to the home of the Sun-god. He asked the birds, but though they flew far they were likewise in ignorance of the road thither. At last he met a wolverine who told him that he had been there himself, and promised to set him on the way. For a long and weary season they marched onward, until at length they came to a great water, too broad and too deep to cross.

As Scar-face sat despondent on the bank bemoaning his situation, two beautiful swans advanced from the water and, requesting him to sit on their backs, bore him across in safety. Landing him on the other side, they showed him which way to take and left him. He had not walked far when he saw a bow and arrows lying on the ground before him. But Scar-face was punctilious and would not pick them up because they did not belong to him. Not long afterward he encountered a beautiful youth of handsome form and smiling aspect.

"I have lost a bow and arrows," he said to Scar-face. "Have you seen them?"

Scar-face told him that he had seen them a little way back, and the handsome youth praised him for his honesty in not appropriating them. He further asked him where he was bound for.

"I am seeking the Sun in his home," replied the Indian, "and I believe that I am not far from my destination."

"You are right," replied the youth. "I am the son of the Sun, Apisirahts, the Morning Star, and I will lead you to the presence of my noble father."

They walked onward for a little time, and then Apisirahts pointed out a great lodge, glorious with golden light and decorated with art more curious than any that Scar-face had ever beheld. At the entrance stood a beautiful woman, the mother of Morning Star. She was Kokomikis, the Moon-goddess, and she welcomed the footsore Indian with kindness.

The Chase of the Savage Birds

Then the great Sun-god appeared, wondrous in his strength and beauty as the mighty planet over which he ruled. He, too, greeted Scar-face kindly, and requested him to be his guest and to hunt with his son. Scar-face and the youth gladly set out for the chase. But on departing the Sun-god warned them not to venture near the Great Water, as there dwelt savage birds which might slay Morning Star.

Scar-face tarried with the Sun, his wife and child, fearful of asking his boon too speedily, and desiring to make as sure as possible of its being granted.

One day when he and Morning Star were hunting as usual, the youth stole away, for he wished to slay the savage birds of which his father had spoken. But Scar-face followed, rescued the lad in imminent peril, and killed the monsters. The Sun was grateful to him for having saved his son from a terrible death, and asked him for what reason he had sought his lodge. Scar-face acquainted him with the circumstances of his love for the chief's daughter and of his quest. At once the Sun-god granted his desire.

"Return to the woman you love so much," he said, "return and make her yours. And as a sign that it is my will that she should be your wife, I make you whole."

With a motion of his bright hand the deity removed the unsightly scar. On quitting the Sun-country the god, his wife and son presented Scar-face with many fine gifts, and showed him a short route by which to return to Earth-land once more.

Scar-face soon reached his home. When he sought his chief's daughter she did not know him at first, so rich was the gleaming attire he had obtained in the Sun-country. But when she at last recognized him she fell upon his breast with a glad cry. That same day she was made his wife. The happy pair raised a medicine lodge to the Sun-god, and henceforth Scar-face was called Smooth-face.

THE TALE OF THE PURSUING HEAD

A poor Indian who had a wife and two children lived in the greatest poverty on roots and berries. This man had a dream in which he heard a voice command him to procure a large spider-web, which he was to hang on the trail of the animals where they passed through the forest; by means of this trap he would obtain plenty of food. This he did, and on returning to the place in which he had hung the web he found deer and rabbits entangled in its magical meshes. These he killed for food, and after this time he had no difficulty in obtaining meat with which to feed his family.

Returning with his game on his shoulders one morning, he discovered his wife perfuming herself with sweet pine, which she burned over the fire. He suspected that she was making herself attractive for the benefit of someone else, but, preserving silence, he told her that on the following day he would set his spider-web at a greater distance, as the game in the neighbouring forest was beginning to know the trap too well. Accordingly on the next morning he went farther afield, and caught a deer, which he cut up, carrying part of its meat back with him to his lodge. He then told his wife where the remainder of the carcass was to be found, and asked her to go and fetch it.

His wife, however, was not without her own suspicions, and, concluding that she was being watched by her husband, she halted at the top of the nearest hill and looked back to see if he was following her. But he was sitting where she had left him, so she proceeded on her way. When she was quite out of sight the Indian himself climbed the hill, and, seeing that she was not in the vicinity, returned to the camp.

The Indian inquired of his children where their mother went to gather

Algonquian Man and Woman Eating by John White, 1585. Painted in the village of Secotan, the couple are eating boiled hominy.

Cree robe of elkskin with the milk teeth of the elk, a popular ornament, hung from thongs attached to beaded discs, and a band of beadwork in Crow style.

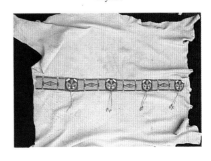

Rattlesnake. Unique to the Americas, the rattlesnake can be found from Canada southwards. (Illustration from Mark Catesby, *The Natural History of Carolina, Florida and the Bahama Islands*, 1731–43.)

firewood, and they pointed in the direction of a large patch of dead timber. Proceeding to the clump of leafless trees that the children had indicated, the man instituted a thorough search, and after a while discovered a den of rattlesnakes. Now it was one of these reptiles with which his wife was in love, so the Indian, in his wrath, gathered fragments of dry wood and set the whole plantation in a blaze. Then he returned to his lodge and told his children what he had done, at the same time warning them that their mother would be very wrathful, and would probably attempt to kill them all.

He further said that he would wait for her return, but that the children had better run away, and that he would provide them with three things which they would find of use. He then handed to the children a stick, a stone and a bunch of moss, which they were to throw behind them one by one should their mother pursue them.

The children at once ran away, and their father hung the magical spider-web over the door of the lodge. Meanwhile the woman had seen the blaze made by the dry timber-patch from a considerable distance, and in great anger at what her husband had done she turned and ran back to the lodge. Attempting to enter it, she was at once entangled in the meshes of the spider-web.

She struggled violently, however, and succeeded in getting her head through the opening, whereupon her husband severed it from her shoulders with his stone axe. He then ran out of the lodge and down the valley, hotly pursued by the woman's body, while her head rolled along the ground in chase of the children. The latter soon spotted the grisly object rolling along in their tracks at a great speed, and one of them quickly threw the stick behind him as he had been told to do. Instantly a dense forest sprang up in their rear, which for a space retarded their horrible pursuer. The children made considerable headway, but eventually the severed head caught up with them again. It made its appearance gnashing its teeth in a frenzy of rage and rolling its eyes horribly, while it shrieked out threats which caused the children's blood to turn to water. And again they sought to delay its progress.

The other boy threw the stone which he had been given behind him, and instantly a great mountain sprang up which occupied the land from sea to sea, so that the progress of the head was quite barred. It could perceive no means of overcoming this immense barrier, until it encountered two rams feeding. The head asked them to make a way for it through the mountain, telling them that if they would do so it would marry the chief of the sheep. The rams made a valiant effort to meet this request, and again and again fiercely rushed at the mountain, till their horns were split and broken and they could butt no longer.

The head, which was by now growing impatient, called upon a colony of ants which dwelt in the neighbourhood to tunnel a passage through the obstacle, and offered, if they were successful, to marry the chief ant as a recompense for their labours. The insects at once took up the task, and toiled incessantly until they had made a tunnel big enough for the head to roll through the mountain.

The children were still running, but felt that the head had not abandoned pursuit. At last, after a long interval, they observed it rolling after them, evidently as fresh as ever. The child who had the bunch of moss

A colony of ants "toiled incessantly until they had made a tunnel". (Illustration from Mark Catesby, The Natural History of Carolina, Florida and the Bahama Islands, 1731–43.)

"An immense strait separated the children from the land." The Columbia River at Crown Point, Oregon.

now wet it and wrung out the water over their trail, and immediately an immense strait separated them from the land where they had been but a moment before. The head, unable to stop, fell into this great water and was drowned.

The children, seeing that their danger was past, made a raft and sailed back to the land from which they had come. Landing there, they then journeyed eastward through many countries, peopled by many different tribes of Indians, in order to reach their own territory. When they arrived there they found it occupied by tribes unknown to them, so they resolved to separate, one going north and the other south.

As for the mother's body, it continued to chase her husband, and is still following him, for she is the Moon and he is the Sun. If she succeeds in catching him she will slay him, and night will reign for evermore, but as long as he is able to evade her day and night will continue to follow one another.

THE DOG AND THE STICK

There was once a great famine among the Blackfeet. For months no buffaloes were killed, and the weaker members of the tribe dropped off, one by one, while even the strong braves and hunters began to sink under the prolonged deprivation. The chief, in despair, prayed that the creator, Nápi, would send them food. Nápi, meanwhile, was far away in the south, painting the plumage of the birds in gorgeous tints. Nevertheless he heard the voice of the chief across the distance, and hastened northward.

"Who has summoned me?" he demanded.

"It was I," said the chief, humbly. "My people are starving, and unless relief comes soon I fear we must all die for lack of anything to eat."

"You shall have food," answered Nápi. "I will provide game for you."

Taking with him the chief's son, Nápi travelled toward the west. As

"They crossed the Sweet Grass Hills which Napi had made." The Madison River Valley, south of Bozeman, Montana.

The Buffalo Hunt under the Wolf Skin Mask by George Catlin, 1832–33. Before Europeans introduced the horse, hunting large prey required great cunning and skill. (National Museum of American Art.)

they went the youth prayed earnestly to the Sun, the Moon and the Morning Star, but his companion rebuked his impatience and bade him hold his peace. They crossed the Sweet Grass Hills which Nápi had made from huge handfuls of herbage, and where he loved to rest. Still there was no sign of game. At length they reached a little lodge by the side of a river, and Nápi called a halt.

"There dwells the cause of your misfortunes," said he. "He who lives in that lodge is the Buffalo-stealer. He it is who has taken all the herds from the prairies, so that there is none left."

To further his plan, Nápi took the shape of a dog, and turned the youth into a stick. Not long afterward the little son of Buffalo-stealer was passing that way, and immediately desired to take the little dog home with him.

"Very well," said his mother. "Take that stick and drive it to the lodge."

But the boy's father frowned angrily.

"I do not like the look of the beast," he said. "Send it away."

The boy refused to part with the dog, and his mother wanted the stick to gather roots with, so the father was obliged to give way. Still he did not show any good-will to the dog. The following day he left the lodge, and in a short time returned with a buffalo, which he skinned and prepared for cooking. His wife, who was in the woods gathering berries, came home towards evening, and at her husband's bidding cooked part of the buffalo-meat. The little boy incurred his father's anger again by giving a piece of meat to the dog.

"Have I not told you," cried Buffalo-stealer irately, "that he is an evil thing? Do not touch him."

That night when all was silent, Nápi and the chief's son resumed their human form and supped off the buffalo-meat.

Cree tepees typically had their fireplaces in the centre with a smoke hole above. (Illustration from Edward Curtis, *The North American Indian*, 1907–30.)

"It is Buffalo-stealer who keeps the herds from coming near the Blackfeet camp," said Nápi. "Wait till morning and see."

In the morning they were once more dog and stick. When the woman and her child awoke, they set off for the woods again, the former taking the stick to dig for roots, the latter calling for his little dog to accompany him. Alas! When they reached the spot they had fixed upon for root-gathering operations, both dog and stick had vanished! And this was the reason for their disappearance: as the dog was trotting through the wood he had observed an opening like the mouth of a cavern, all but concealed by the thick undergrowth, and in the aperture he perceived a buffalo. His short, sharp barking attracted the attention of the stick, which promptly wriggled snake-wise after him. Within the cavern were great herds of deer and buffalo, enough to provide the Blackfeet with food for years and years. Nápi the dog ran among them, barking, and the animals were driven out to the prairie.

When Buffalo-stealer returned to the cave and discovered his loss, his wrath knew no bounds. He asked his wife and son what they knew about it, but they denied all knowledge of the affair.

"Then," said he, "it is that wretched little dog of yours. Where is he now?"

But the child could not tell him.

"We lost him in the woods," said he.

"I shall kill him," shouted the man, "and I shall break the stick as well!"

Nápi overheard the threat, and clung to the long hair of an old buffalo. He advised the stick to conceal itself in the buffalo's hair also, and so the twain escaped unnoticed from the cave. Once again they took the form of men, and drove a herd of buffalo to the Blackfeet camp, while Buffalo-stealer and his family sought them in vain.

The people met them with delighted acclamations, and the famine was at an end. Yet there were still some difficulties in the way, for when they tried to get the herd into the enclosure, a large grey bird so frightened the animals with its dismal note that they refused to enter. This occurred so often that Nápi suspected that the grey bird was no other than Buffalo-stealer. Changing himself into an otter, he lay by the side of a river and pretended to be dead. The greedy bird saw what he thought to be a dead otter and pounced upon it, whereupon Nápi seized him by the leg and bore him off to the camp. By way of punishment he was tied over the smoke-hole of the wigwam, where his grey feathers soon became black and his life a burden to him.

"Spare me!" he cried. "Let me return to my wife and child. They will surely starve."

His piteous appeals moved the heart of Nápi, and he let him go but not without an admonition.

"Go," said he, "and hunt for food, that you may support your wife and child. But do not take more than you need, or you shall die."

The bird did as he was bidden. But to this day the feathers of the raven are black, and not grey.

THE STORY OF KUTOYIS

There once lived on the banks of the Missouri an old couple who had one daughter, their only child. When she grew to be a woman she had a suitor who was cruel and overbearing, but as she loved him her parents offered no opposition to their marriage. Indeed, they gave the bride the best part of their possessions for a dowry, so that she and her husband were rich, while her father and mother lived in a poor lodge and had very little to eat. The wicked son-in-law took advantage of their kindness in every way. He forced the old man to accompany him on his hunting expeditions, and then refused to share the game with him. Sometimes one would kill a buffalo and sometimes the other, but always it was the younger man who got the best of the meat and who made himself robes and moccasins from the hide.

Because of this treatment the aged couple were nearly perishing from

The Missouri River (right). Over 3,700 kilometres long, the Missouri gets its name from an Indian word meaning "people of the long canoes".

In the kettle was a little boy. Blackfeet child by George Catlin. (Illustration from *Letters on the North American Indians*, 1841.)

cold and hunger. Only when her unkind husband was out hunting would the daughter venture to carry a morsel of meat to her parents.

On one occasion the younger man called in his overbearing way to his father-in-law, bidding him help in a buffalo-hunt. The old man, reduced almost to a skeleton, was too much afraid of the tyrant to venture to disobey him, so he accompanied him in the chase. Before long they encountered a fine buffalo, whereupon both drew their bows and fired. But it was the arrow of the elder man which pierced the animal and brought it to the ground. The old man set himself to skin the buffalo, for his son-in-law never shared in these tasks, but left them to his companion. While he was thus occupied, the old man observed a drop of blood on one of his arrows which had fallen to the ground.

Thinking that even a drop of blood was better than nothing, he replaced the arrow in its quiver and set off home. As it happened, no more of the buffalo than that fell to his share, the rest being appropriated by his son-in-law.

On his return the old man called to his wife to heap fuel on the fire and put on the kettle. She, thinking he had brought home some buffalo-meat, hastened to do his bidding. She waited curiously till the water in the kettle had boiled, then to her surprise she saw him place in it an arrow with a drop of blood on it.

How Kutoyis Was Born

"Why do you do that?" she asked.

"Something will come of it," he replied. "My spirit tells me so."

They waited in silence.

Then a strange sound was heard in their lonely little lodge—the crying of a child. Half fearfully, half curiously, the old couple lifted the lid of the kettle, and there within was a little baby boy.

"He shall bring us good luck," said the old Indian.

They called the child Kutoyis—that is, "Drop of Blood"—and wrapped him up as is customary with Indian babies.

"Let us tell our son-in-law," said the old man, "that the baby is a little girl, and he will let it live. If we say it is a boy he will surely kill it."

Kutoyis became a great favourite in the little lodge to which he had come. He was always laughing, and his merriment won the hearts of the old people. One day, while they thought him much too young to speak, they were astonished to hear his voice.

"Lash me up and hang me from the lodge pole," said he, "and I shall become a man."

When they had recovered from the astonishment, they lashed him to the lodge pole. In a moment he had burst the lashings and grown before their eyes into a tall, strong man. Looking round the lodge, which seemed scarcely large enough to hold him, Kutoyis perceived that there was no food about.

"Give me some arrows," said he, "and I will bring you food."

"We have no arrows," replied the old man, "only four arrow-heads."

Kutoyis fetched some wood, from which he cut a fine bow and shafts to fit the flint arrow-heads. He begged the old Indian to lead him to a good hunting-ground, and when he had done so they quickly killed a magnificent buffalo.

Meanwhile the old Indian had told Kutoyis how badly his son-in-law had treated him, and as they were skinning the buffalo who should pass by but the subject of their conversation. Kutoyis hid behind the dead animal to see what would happen, and a moment later the angry voice of the son-in-law was heard.

Getting no reply, the cowardly hunter fitted an arrow to his bow and shot it at his father-in-law. Enraged at the cruel act, Kutoyis rose from his hiding-place behind the dead buffalo and fired all his arrows at the young man, whom he slew. He afterward gave food in plenty to the old man and his wife, and bade them return to their home. They were delighted to find themselves once more free from persecution, but their daughter wept so much that finally Kutoyis asked her whether she would have another husband or whether she wished to follow her first spouse to

Blackfeet warrior on horseback.
(Illustration by Karl Bodmer from
M. A. P. Wied-Neuwied, *Voyage dans
l'intérieur de l'Amérique du Nord*,
1840–43.)

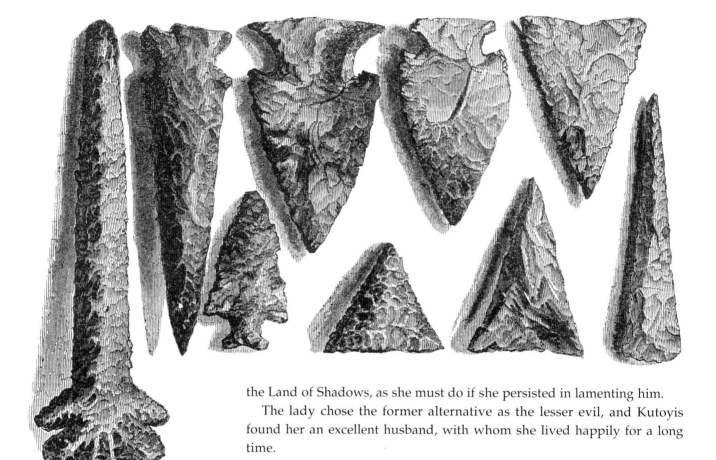

Flint arrow heads. (Illustration from
H. R. Schoolcraft, *Narrative Journal of
Travels from Detroit North-west through
the Great Chain of American Lakes,*
1821.)

the Land of Shadows, as she must do if she persisted in lamenting him.

The lady chose the former alternative as the lesser evil, and Kutoyis found her an excellent husband, with whom she lived happily for a long time.

Kutoyis on his Travels

At length Kutoyis tired of his monotonous life, and desired to see more of the world. So his host directed him to a distant village, where he was welcomed by two old women. They set before their handsome guest the best fare at their disposal, which was buffalo-meat of a rather unattractive appearance.

"Is there no good meat?" queried Kutoyis.

The old women explained that one of the lodges was occupied by a fierce bear, who seized upon all the good meat and left only the dry, poor sort for his neighbours. Without hesitation Kutoyis went out and killed a buffalo calf, which he presented to the women, desiring them to place the best parts of the meat in a prominent position outside the lodge, where the big bear could not fail to see it.

This they did, and sure enough one of the bear-cubs shortly passed by and seized the meat. Kutoyis, who had been lying in wait, rushed out and hit the animal as hard as he could. The cub carried his tale of woe to his father, and the big bear, growling threats of vengeance, gathered his whole family round him and rushed to the lodge of the old women, intending to kill the bold hunter.

However, Kutoyis was more than a match for all of them, and very soon the bears were slain. Still he was unsatisfied, and longed for further adventures.

"Tell me," said he, "where shall I find another village?"

"There is a village by the Big River," said the old women, "but you must not go there for a wicked woman dwells in it who wrestles with and slays all those who approach."

No sooner did Kutoyis hear this than he determined to seek the village, for his mission was to destroy evil beings who were a danger to his fellow-men. So in spite of the dissuasions of the old women he departed.

As he had been warned, the woman came out of her lodge on the approach of the stranger and invited him to wrestle with her.

"I cannot," said he, pretending to be frightened.

The woman mocked and jeered at him, while he made various excuses, but all the time he was observing how the land lay. When he drew nearer he saw that she had covered the ground with sharp flints, over which she had strewn grass to hide them. At last he said: "Very well, I will wrestle with you."

It was no wonder that she had killed many braves, for she was very strong. But Kutoyis was still stronger. With all her skill she could not throw him, and at last she grew tired, and was herself thrown on the sharp flints, on which she bled to death. The people rejoiced greatly when they heard of the wicked woman's death, and Kutoyis was universally acclaimed as a hero.

Kutoyis did many other great deeds before he departed to the Shadowland, and when he went he left sorrow in many lodges.

The Columbia River, with Rocky Mountains, near Fairmont, British Columbia, on the western fringes of the Algonquian-speaking area.

CHAPTER 2

IROQUOIS MYTHS AND LEGENDS

A hunter, caught in a heavy thunder-shower, took refuge in the woods. Crouching under the shelter of a great tree, he became aware of a mysterious voice which urged him to follow it. He was conscious of a sensation of slowly rising from the earth, and he soon found himself gazing downward from a point near the clouds, the height of many trees from the ground. He was surrounded by beings who had all the appearance of men, with one among them who seemed to be their chief.

They asked him to cast his eyes toward the earth and tell them whether he could see a huge water-serpent. When he said he was unable to catch sight of the monster, the chief anointed his eyes with a sacred ointment, which gave him supernatural sight and permitted him to behold a dragon-like shape in the watery depths far below him.

The chief commanded one of his warriors to dispatch the monster. When arrow after arrow failed to transfix it, he turned to the hunter.

"Will you show us your skill as an archer?" he asked.

Drawing his bow, the man took careful aim. The arrow whizzed through the air and down into the depths of the water, and was speedily lost to sight. But, although nothing could at first be seen, a terrible commotion soon arose in the lake below.

Pierced by the arrow, the body of the monstrous serpent began leaping from the blood-stained water in dreadful writhings and contortions. So appalling was the din that rose up to them that even the heavenly beings by whom the hunter was surrounded fell into a great trembling at the noise of it.

Then gradually the tempest of sound started to subside, the huge bulk of the mortally wounded serpent sank back into the lake, the surface of the water became gradually more still, and finally all was peace once more. The chief turned again to the hunter.

"We are grateful for the service you have rendered," he said. "Now the serpent is dead we shall conduct you back to the earth."

Thus was man first brought into contact with the beneficent heavenly beings, and thus did he learn the existence of a power which would protect him from forces unfriendly to humanity.

Iroquois beaded sash and bag, emblem of a high-ranking tribal official. The dark background is typical of such work for the time around 1850 when these were made.

The shaman or medicine man (opposite) used a combination of herbal remedies and magical formulas. (Illustration from Edward Curtis, *The North American Indian*, 1907–30.)

Niagara Falls stands at the heart of Iroquois territory. (Illustration by Karl Bodmer from M. A. P. Wied-Neuwied, *Voyage dans l'intérieur de l'Amérique du Nord*, 1840–43.)

THE THUNDERERS

Once, in early Iroquois days, three braves set out upon an expedition. After they had journeyed for some time a misfortune occurred, one of their number breaking his leg. The others made a litter, following Indian custom, with the object of carrying him back to his home. Retracing their steps, they came to a range of high mountains, the steep slopes of which taxed their strength to the utmost. To rest themselves they placed the disabled man on the ground and withdrew a short distance.

"Why should we be thus burdened with a wounded man?" said one to the other.

"You speak truly," was the rejoinder. "Why should we, indeed, since his hurt has come upon him by reason of his own carelessness?"

As they spoke their eyes met in a meaningful glance, and one of them pointed to a deep hole, or pit opening, in the side of the mountain at a little distance from the place where they were sitting. Returning to the injured man, they raised him as if about to proceed on the journey, and when passing the brink of the pit suddenly hurled him into it with great force. Then, without loss of time, they set their faces homeward. When they arrived in camp they reported that their comrade had died of wounds received in fight, but that he had not fallen into the enemy's hands, having received careful attention from them in his dying moments and honourable burial. The unfortunate man's aged mother was prostrate with grief at the sad news, but was somewhat relieved to think that her son had been kindly ministered to at the end.

When the brave who had been thrown into the pit regained his senses after his severe fall, he perceived a man of venerable aspect solicitously bending over him. When this person saw that the young man had regained consciousness, he asked him what had been the intention of his comrades in so cruelly casting him into that abyss. The young man replied that his fellows had become tired of carrying him and had thus rid themselves of him. The old hermit—for so he seemed to be—made a hasty examination of the Indian's injuries, and announced that he would speedily cure him, on one condition. The other pledged his word to accept this, whatever it might be, whereupon the recluse told him that all he required was that he should hunt for him and bring home to him such game as he should slay. To this the brave gave a ready assent. The old man lost no time in performing his part of the bargain. He applied herbs to his injuries and assiduously tended his guest, who made a speedy and satisfactory recovery.

The grateful warrior, one more able to follow the chase, brought home many trophies of his skill as a hunter to the cave on the mountainside, and soon the pair had formed a strong attachment. One day, when in the forest, the warrior encountered an enormous bear, which he succeeded in slaying after a desperate struggle. As he was pondering how best he could remove it to the cave he became aware of a murmur of voices behind him, and glancing round he saw three men, or beings in the shape of men, clad in strange translucent garments, standing near. In reply to his question as to what brought them there, they told him that they were the Thunderers, or people of Hi'nun, whose mission it was to keep the earth in good order for the benefit of humanity, and to slay or destroy anything hostile to mankind. They told him that the old man with whom he had been residing was by no means the sort of person he seemed to think, and that they had come to earth with the express intention of bringing about his destruction. In this they requested the warrior's assistance, and promised him that if he would vouchsafe it he would speedily be transported back to his mother's lodge.

Overjoyed at this proposal, the hunter did not have qualms about returning to the cave to tell the hermit that he had killed the bear, which he wished his help in bringing home. The old man seemed very uneasy, and begged him to examine the sky and tell him whether he perceived the least sign of clouds. The young brave reassured him and told him that not a cloud was to be seen, whereupon, emerging from his shelter, he made for the spot where the bear was lying. Hastily picking up the carcass, he requested his companion to place it on his shoulders, which the young man did, expressing surprise at the older man's great strength. He had proceeded with his burden for some distance when a terrific clap of thunder burst from the menacing black clouds which had speedily gathered overhead. In great terror the old man threw down his load and started to run with an agility which belied his years, but when a second peal broke forth he suddenly assumed the shape of a gigantic porcupine, which dashed through the undergrowth, discharging its quills like arrows as it ran. A veritable hail of thunderbolts now crashed down upon the creature's spiny back. As it reached the entrance to the cave, one thunderbolt larger than the rest struck it with such tremendous force that the porcupine rolled dead into its den.

Then the Thunderers swooped down from the sky in triumph, mightily pleased at the death of their victim. The young hunter asked them to carry out the promise they had made him to transport him back to his

They made a litter. Without the wheel, Native Americans transported goods and people by means of a dragging system. (Illustration from George Catlin, *Letters on the North American Indians*, 1841.)

Iroquois model of warrior with mask. The mask was not intended to disguise the wearer but to symbolize the spirit forces that represented mythological beings.

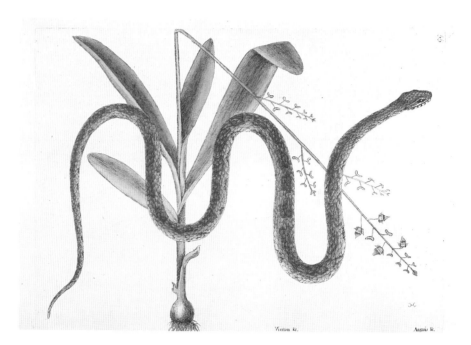

Corn snake (right). (Illustration from Mark Catesby, *The Natural History of Carolina, Florida and the Bahama Islands*, 1731–43.)

The old man was terrified by the thunderclap. (Illustration from T. L. McKenney, *Travels among the Northern and Southern Indians*, 1846.)

mother's lodge, so, having fastened cloud-wings on his shoulders, they speedily brought him thither, carrying him carefully through the air and depositing him just outside the hut. The widow was delighted to see her son, whom she had believed to be long dead, and the Thunderers were so pleased with the assistance he had lent them that they asked him to accompany them in their monster-destroying mission every spring.

The young man assented, and on one of these expeditions flew earthwards to drink from a certain pool. When he rejoined his companions they observed that the water with which his lips were moist had caused them to shine as if smeared with oil. At their request he indicated the pool from which he had drunk, and they informed him that in its depths there dwelt a monster for which they had searched for years. With that they hurled a great thunderbolt into the pool, which immediately dried up, revealing an immense grub, of the species which destroys standing crops. The monster was, indeed, the King of Grubs, and his death set back the conspiracies of his kind for many generations. The youth subsequently returned to earth, and having told the members of his tribe the services which Hi'nun had performed on their behalf, they considered it fitting to institute a special worship of the deity, and, in fact, to make him supreme god of their nation. Even today many Iroquois allude to Hi'nun as their grandfather, and show extraordinary respect at the mention of his name.

THE ANIMALS' MEDICINE

Over two hundred years ago an Indian went alone into the woods on a hunting expedition. One night while he lay asleep in his solitary camp, he was awakened by a great noise of singing and drum-beating of the kind that is heard at festivals. Starting up, he made his way to the place from which the sounds came, and although he could not see anyone there he observed a heap of corn and a large squash vine with three squashes on it, and three ears of corn which lay apart from the rest. The next day, feeling very uneasy, he once more pursued his hunting operations, and when night came again laid himself down to rest. But his sleep was destined to be broken yet a second time, and awaking, he perceived a man bending over him, who said in menacing tones:

"Beware: what you saw was sacred. You deserve to die."

A rustling among the branches denoted the presence of a number of people, who, after some hesitation, gathered round the hunter, and informed him that they would pardon his curiosity and would tell him their secret. "The great medicine for wounds," said the man who had first awakened him, "is squash and corn. Come with me and I will teach you how to make and apply it."

With these words he led the hunter to the spot at which he had surprised the medicine-making operations on the previous night, where he beheld a great fire and a strange-looking laurel bush, which seemed to be made of iron. Chanting a weird song, the people circled slowly round the bush to the accompaniment of a rattling of gourd shells. When the hunter asked them to explain this procedure, one of them heated a stick and thrust it right through his cheek. He immediately applied some of their medicine to the wound, so that it instantly healed. Having thus demonstrated the power of the drug, they sang a tune which they called the "medicine-song," which their pupil learnt by heart.

The hunter then turned to depart, and all at once he saw that the beings who surrounded him were not human, as he had thought, but animals—foxes bears, and beavers—who fled as he looked at them. Surprised and even terrifed at the turn matters had taken, he made his way homeward with all speed, thinking over the prescription which the strange beings had given him the while. They had told him to take one stalk of corn, to dry the cob and pound it very fine, then to take one squash, cut it up and pound it, and to mix the whole with water from a running stream, near its source. This prescription he used with very great success among his people, and it proved the origin of the great medicine of the Senecas. Once a year; at the season when the deer changes his coat,

Birch bark container, Iroquois or Chippewa. Birch bark was used for a wide variety of domestic utensils, including buckets, dishes and storage vessels.

A certain tribe of the Senecas lives on the shores of Lake Erie (left). The Senecas, like many Iroquois people, sustained themselves by intensive fishing and horticulture.

they prepared it as the forest folk did, singing the strange song and dancing round it to the rhythmic accompaniment of the gourd shell rattles, while they burnt tobacco to the gods.

PROMISE OF VENGEANCE

A certain tribe of the Senecas had settled on the shores of Lake Erie when they were surprised by their ancient enemies the Illinois, and in spite of a stout resistance many of them were slain, and a woman and a boy taken prisoner. When the victors halted for the night they built a great fire, and proceeded to celebrate their success by singing triumphant songs, in which they commanded the boy to join them. The lad pretended that he did not know their language, but said that he would sing their song in his own tongue, to which his captors assented. Instead of a hymn in their praise, however, he sang a song of vengeance, in which he vowed that if he were spared all of them would lose their scalps. A few days afterwards the woman became so exhausted that she could walk no farther, so the Illinois slew her. But before she died she extracted a promise from the boy that he would avenge her, and would never cease to be a Seneca.

In a few days they arrived at the Illinois camp, where a council was held to consider the fate of the captive youth. Some were for instantly putting him to death, but their chief ruled that should he be able to live through their tortures he would be worthy of becoming an Illinois. They seized the wretched lad and held his bare feet to the glowing council-fire, then after piercing them they told him to run a race. He bounded forward and ran so swiftly that he soon gained the Great House of the tribe, where he seated himself upon a wildcat skin.

Another council was held, and the Illinois braves agreed that the lad possessed high courage and would make a great warrior, but others argued and it was finally decided that he should be burnt at the stake. As he was about to perish in this manner an aged warrior suggested that if he were able to withstand their last torture he should be permitted to live. Accordingly he held the unfortunate boy underwater in a pool until only a spark of life remained in him, but he survived and became an Illinois warrior.

Years passed, and the boy reached manhood and married a chief's daughter. His strength and endurance became proverbial, but the warriors of the tribe of his adoption would never permit him to take part in their warlike expeditions. At length a raid against the Senecas was mooted, and he begged so hard to be allowed to accompany the braves that at last they consented. Indeed, so great was their admiration of the skill with which he outlined a plan of campaign that they made him chief of the expedition. For many days the party marched toward the Seneca country, but when at last they neared it their scouts reported that there were no signs of the tribe, and that the Senecas must have quitted their territory. Their leader, however, proposed to go in search of the enemy himself, along with another warrior of the tribe.

When the pair had gone five or six miles, the leader said to his com-

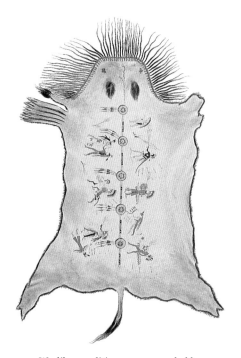

Warlike expeditions were recorded by Plains tribes in pictograms. (Illustration by Karl Bodmer from M. A. P. Wied-Neuwied, *Voyage dans l'intérieur de l'Amérique du Nord*, 1840–43.)

panion that it would be better if they separated, as they would then be able to cover more ground. Passing on to where he knew he would find the Senecas, he warned them of the danger and arranged that an ambush of his kinsfolk should lie in wait for the Illinois.

Returning to the Illinois camp, he reported that he had seen nothing, but that he well remembered the Seneca hiding-place. He asked to be given the bravest warriors, and assured the council that he would soon bring them the scalps of their foes. Suspecting nothing, they assented to his proposal, and he was followed from the camp by the flower of the Illinois tribe, all unaware that five hundred Senecas awaited them in the valley. The youth led his men right into the heart of the ambush; then, pretending to miss his footing, he fell. This was the signal for the Senecas to rise on every side. Yelling their war-cry, they rushed from their shelter and fell on the terrified Illinois, who gave way on every side. The slaughter was immense. Vengeance nerved the arms of the Seneca braves, and of three hundred Illinois, only two escaped. The leader of the expedition was borne in triumph to the Seneca village, where he told the tribe the story of his capture and long-meditated revenge. He became a great chief among his people, and even to this day his name is uttered by them with honour and reverence.

THE BOY WHO WENT WEST

In the heart of the wilderness there lived an old woman and her little grandson. The two found no lack of occupation from day to day, the woman busying herself with cooking and cleaning and the boy with shooting and

Hurons and French attacking an Onondaga village. Europeans exploited existing conflicts between tribes for their own ends. (Canada House.)

hunting. The grandmother frequently spoke of the time when the child would grow up and go out into the world.

"Always go to the east," she would say. "Never go to the west, for there lies danger."

But what the danger was she would not tell him, in spite of his persistent questioning. Other boys went west, he thought to himself, why should not he? Nevertheless, his grandmother made him promise that he would not go west.

Years passed by, and the child grew to be a man, though he still retained the curiosity and high spirits of his boyhood. His frequent inquiries drew from the old grandmother a reluctant explanation of her warning.

"In the west", said she, "there dwells a being who is anxious to do us harm. If he sees you it will mean death for both of us."

This statement, instead of frightening the young Indian, only strengthened in him a secret resolution he had formed to go west on the first opportunity. Not that he wished to bring any misfortune on his poor old grandmother, any more than on himself, but he trusted to his strong arm and clear head to deliver them from their enemy. So with a smile on his lips he set off to the west.

Toward evening he came to a lake, where he rested. He had not been there long when he heard a voice saying: "Aha, my fine fellow, I see you!"

The youth looked all round him, and up into the sky above, but he saw no one.

"I am going to send a hurricane," the mysterious voice continued, "to break your grandmother's hut to pieces. How will you like that?"

"Oh, very well," answered the young man gaily. "We are always in need of firewood, and now we shall have plenty."

"Go home and see," the voice said mockingly. "I daresay you will not like it so well."

Nothing daunted, the young adventurer retraced his steps. As he neared home a great wind sprang up, seeming to tear the very trees out by the roots.

"Make haste!" cried the grandmother from the doorway. "We shall both be killed!"

When she had drawn him inside and shut the door, she scolded him heartily for his disobedience, and bewailed the fate before them. The young man soothed her fears, saying: "Dont cry, grandmother. We shall turn the lodge into a rock, and so we shall be saved."

Having some skill in magic, he did as he had said, and the hurricane passed harmlessly over their heads. When it had ceased they emerged from their retreat, and found an abundance of firewood all round them.

Next day the youth was on the point of setting off toward the west once more, but the urgent entreaties of his grandmother moved him to proceed eastward—for a time. Directly he was out of sight of the lodge he turned his face once more to the west. Arrived at the lake, he heard the voice once more, though its owner was still invisible.

"I am going to send a great hailstorm on your grandmother's hut," it said. "What do you think of that?"

He tranformed the hut into a hollow rock.
Doric Rock, Lake Superior. (Illustration
from T. L. MacKenney, *Sketches of a
Tour of the Lakes*, 1827.)

"Oh," was the response, "I think I should like it. I have always wanted a bundle of spears."

"Go home and see," said the voice.

Away the youth went through the woods. The sky became darker and darker as he neared his home, and just as he was within a bowshot of the little hut a fierce hailstorm broke, and he thought he would be killed before he reached shelter.

"Alas!" cried the old woman when he was safely indoors, "we shall be destroyed this time. How can we save ourselves?"

Again the young man exercised his magic powers, and transformed the frail hut into a hollow rock, upon which the shafts of the hailstorm spent themselves in vain. At last the sky cleared, the lodge resumed its former shape and the young man saw a multitude of sharp, beautiful spear-heads on the ground.

"I will get poles," said he, "to fit to them for fishing."

When he returned in a few minutes with the poles he found that the spears had vanished.

"Where are my beautiful spears?" he asked his grandmother.

"They were only ice-spears," she replied. "They have all melted away."

The young Indian was greatly disappointed, and wondered how he could avenge himself on the being who had played him this malicious trick.

"Be warned in time," said the aged grandmother, shaking her head at him. "Take my advice and leave him alone."

But the youth's adventurous spirit forced him to see the end of the matter, so he took a stone and tied it round his neck for a charm, and sought the lake once again. Carefully observing the direction from which the voice proceeded, he saw in the middle of the lake a huge head with a face on every side of it.

"Aha! uncle," he exclaimed, "I see you! How would you like it if the lake dried up?"

"Nonsense!" said the voice angrily, "That will never happen."

"Go home and see," shouted the youth, mimicking the mocking tone the other had adopted on the previous occasions. As he spoke he swung his charmed stone round his head and threw it into the air. As it descended it grew larger and larger, and the moment it entered the lake the water began to boil.

The lad returned home and told his grandmother what he had done.

"It is of no use," said she. "Many have tried to slay him, but all have perished in the attempt."

Next morning our hero went westward again, and found the lake quite dry and the animals in it dead, with the exception of a large green frog, who was in reality the malicious being who had tormented the Indian and his grandmother. A quick blow with a stick put an end to the creature, and the triumphant youth bore the good news to his old grandmother, who from that time was left in peace and quiet.

A large green frog. (Illustration from Mark Catesby, *The Natural History of Carolina, Florida and the Bahama Islands*, 1731–43.)

THE FRIENDLY SKELETON

A little boy living in the woods with his old uncle was warned by him not to go eastward, but to play close to the lodge or walk only toward the west. The child felt a natural curiosity to know what lay in the forbidden direction, and one day took advantage of his uncle's absence on a hunting expedition to wander away to the east. At length he came to a large lake, on the shores of which he stopped to rest. Here he was accosted by a man, who asked him his name and where he lived.

"Come," said the stranger, when he had finished questioning the boy, "let us see who can shoot an arrow the highest."

This they did, and the boy's arrow went much higher than that of his companion.

The stranger then suggested a swimming match.

"Let us see," he said, "who can swim farthest under water without taking a breath."

Again the boy beat his rival, who next proposed that they should sail out to an island in the middle of the lake, to see the beautiful birds that were to be found there. The child readily consented, and they embarked in a curious canoe, which was propelled by three swans harnessed to either side of it. Directly they had taken their seats the man began to sing, and the canoe moved off. In a very short time they had reached the island. Here the little Indian realized that his confidence in his new-found friend was misplaced. The stranger took all his clothes from him, put them in the canoe and jumped in himself, saying:

"Come, swans, let us go home."

The obedient swans set off at a good pace, and soon left the island far

Huron man smoking a pipe (left). In the area around the Great Lakes the pipe was a token of peace and brotherhood. (Illustration from J. F. Latifau, *Moeurs des Sauvages Amériquains*, 1724.)

"You shall find a tobacco-pouch." Except in the Arctic, tobacco was smoked all over North America. (Illustration by Karl Bodmer from M. A. P. Wied-Neuwied, *Voyage dans l'intérieur de l'Amérique du Nord*, 1840–43.)

behind. The boy was very angry at having been so badly used, but when it grew dark his resentment changed to fear, and he sat down and cried with cold and misery. Suddenly he heard a husky voice close at hand, and, looking round, he saw a skeleton on the ground.

"I am very sorry for you," said the skeleton in hoarse tones. "I will do what I can to help you. But first you must do something for me. Go and dig by that tree, and you shall find a tobacco-pouch with some tobacco in it, a pipe and a flint."

The boy did as he was asked, and when he had filled the pipe he lit it and placed it in the mouth of the skeleton. He saw that the latter's body was full of mice, and that the smoke frightened them away.

"There is a man coming tonight with three dogs," said the skeleton. "He is coming to look for you. You must make tracks all over the island, so that they may not find you, and then hide in a hollow tree."

Again the boy obeyed his gaunt instructor, and when he was safely hidden he saw a man come ashore with three dogs. All night they hunted him, but he had made so many tracks that the dogs were confused, and at

Taking bark for canoe making.
(Illustration from the Rev E. R. Young,
*By Canoe and Dog Train among the Cree
and Salteaux Indians, 1903.*)

last the man departed in anger. Next day the trembling boy emerged from his hiding place in the tree and went to the skeleton.

"Tonight," said the latter, "the man who brought you here is coming to drink your blood. You must dig a hole in the sand and hide. When he comes out of the canoe you must enter it. Say, 'Come, swans, let us go home,' and if the man calls you, do not look back."

Everything happened as the skeleton had foretold. The boy hid in the sand, and directly he saw his tormentor step ashore he jumped into the canoe, saying hastily, "Come, swans, let us go home." Then he began to sing as he had heard the man do when they first embarked. In vain the man called him back; he refused to look round. The swans carried the canoe to a cave in a high rock, where the boy found his clothes, as well as a fire and food. When he had donned his garments and satisfied his hunger, he lay down and slept. In the morning he returned to the island, where he found the tyrant, quite dead. The skeleton now commanded him to sail to the east to seek for his sister, whom a fierce tyrant had carried away. He set out eagerly on his new quest, and after three days arrived at the place where his sister was. He lost no time in finding her.

"Come, my sister," said he, "let us flee away together."

"Alas! I cannot," answered the young woman. "A wicked man keeps me here. It is time for him to return home, and he would be sure to catch us. But let me hide you now, and in the morning we shall go away."

So she dug a pit and hid her brother, though not a moment too soon, for the footsteps of her husband were heard approaching the hut. The woman had cooked a kid, and this she placed before the man.

"You have had visitors," he said, seeing his dogs sniffing round uneasily.

"No," was the reply, "I have seen no one but you."

"I shall wait till to-morrow," said the tyrant to himself. "Then I shall kill and eat him." He had already guessed that his wife had not spoken the truth. However, he said nothing more, but waited till morning, when, instead of going to a distant swamp to seek for food, as he pretended to do, he concealed himself at a short distance from the hut and at length saw the brother and sister making for a canoe. They were hardly seated when they saw him running toward them. In his hand he bore a large hook, with which he caught the frail vessel, but the boy broke the hook with a stone, and the canoe darted out on to the lake. The man was at a loss for a moment, and could only shout incoherent threats after the pair. Then an idea occurred to him, and, lying down on the shore, he began to drink the water. This caused the canoe to rush back again, but once more the boy was equal to the occasion. Seizing the large stone with which he had broken the hook, he threw it at the man and slew him, the water at the same time rushing back into the lake. Thus the brother and sister escaped, and in three days they had heartily thanked their benefactor, the skeleton. He, however, had still another task for the young Indian to perform.

"Take your sister home to your uncle's lodge," said he; "then return here yourself, and say to the many bones which you will find on the island, 'Arise,' and they shall come to life again."

When the brother and sister reached their home they found that their old uncle had been grievously lamenting the loss of his nephew, and he was quite overjoyed at seeing them both. On his recommendation they built a large lodge to accommodate the people they were to bring back with them. When it was completed, the youth revisited the island, bade the bones arise, and was delighted to see them obey his bidding and become whole men and women. He led them to the lodge he had built, where they all dwelt happily for a long time.

Woman of Florida, by John White (active 1585-93). White visited the English settlement at Roanoke in Virginia in 1585 and made several detailed watercolours there.

HELP FROM THE PIGMIES

When the Cherokee tribe was dwelling in the swamps of Florida the Iroquois made a practice of swooping down on them and raiding their camps. On one occasion, the raiding party was absent from home for almost two years. On the eve of their return one of their number, a chieftain, fell ill, and the rest of the party were at a loss to know what to do with him.

Obviously, if they carried him home with them he would considerably impede their progress. Besides, there was the possibility that he might not recover, and all their labour would be to no purpose. Thus they debated far into the night, and finally decided to abandon him to his fate and return by themselves. The sick man, unable to stir hand or foot, overheard their decision, but he bore it stoically like an Indian warrior. Nevertheless, when he heard the last swish of their paddles as they crossed the river he could not help thinking of the friends and kindred he would probably never see again.

When the raiders eventually reached home without him they were closely questioned as to the whereabouts of the missing chief, and the enquiries were all the more anxious because the sick man had been a great favourite among his people. The guilty warriors were evasive in their responses. They did not know what had become of their comrade, they said. Possibly he had been lost or killed in Florida.

Meanwhile the sick man lay dying on the banks of the river. Suddenly he heard, quite close at hand, the gentle sound of a canoe. The vessel drew in close to bank and, in full view of the warrior, three pigmy men disembarked. They regarded the stranger with some surprise. At length one who seemed to be the leader advanced and spoke to him, bidding him await their return, and promising to look after him. They were going, he said, to a certain salt-lick, where many curious animals watered, in order to kill some for food.

On the banks of the river. The Ottowa at Vaudreuil by T. Mower Martin from *Canada*, 1907.

Man commenced the wholesale slaughter of the beasts. Attacking the grizzly bear by George Catlin, from *North American Portfolio*, 1844.

The invention of lethal weapons widened the breach between men and animals. Antelope shooting by George Catlin, from *North American Portfolio*, 1844.

When the pigmies arrived at the place they found that no animals were as yet to be seen, but very soon a large buffalo bull came to drink. Immediately a buffalo cow arose from the lick, and when they had satisfied their thirst the two animals lay down on the bank. The pigmies concluded that the time was ripe for killing them, and, drawing their bows, they succeeded in dispatching the buffaloes. Returning to the sick man, they amply fulfilled their promise to take care of him, skilfully tending him until he had made a complete recovery. They then conveyed him to his friends, who now learned that the story told them by the raiders was false. Bitterly indignant at the deception and heartless cruelty of those men who had abandoned the Chieftain, they fell upon them and punished them according to their just deserts.

THE ANIMALS VERSUS MANKIND

In the old days, the members of the animal race were gifted with speech and dwelt happily with the human race, but mankind multiplied so quickly that the animals were crowded into the forests and desert places of the earth, and the old friendship between them was soon forgotten. The breach was farther widened by the invention of lethal weapons, with which man soon commenced the wholesale slaughter of the beasts for the sake of their flesh and skins.

The animals, at first surprised, soon grew angry and resolved upon measures of retaliation. The bear tribe met in council, presided over by the Old White Bear, their chief. After several speakers had denounced mankind for their bloodthirsty tendencies, war was unanimously decided upon, but the lack of weapons was regarded as a serious drawback. However, it was suggested that man's instruments should be turned against himself, and as the bow and arrow were considered to be the principal human agency of destruction, it was resolved to fashion a specimen. A suitable piece of wood was procured, and one of the bears sacrificed himself to

Metal kettles were suspended over the fire by a tripod. Such articles were acquired by the Woodland Indians from the great fur trading companies.

provide gut for a bowstring. When the weapon was completed it was discovered that the claws of the bears spoiled their shooting. One of the bears cut his claws, but the Old White Bear very wisely remarked that without claws they could not climb trees or bring down game, and that were they to cut them off they must all starve.

The deer also met in council, under their chief, the Little Deer. It was decided that those hunters who slew one of their number without asking pardon in a suitable manner should be afflicted with rheumatism. They gave notice of this decision to the nearest settlement of Indians, and instructed them how to appease them when forced by necessity to kill one of the deer-folk.

When a deer was slain by the hunter the Little Deer would run to the spot, and, bending over the blood-stains ask the spirit of the deer if it had heard the prayer of the hunter for pardon. If the reply was 'Yes,' all was well, and the Little Deer would depart, but if the answer was in the negative, he would track the hunter to his cabin and strike him with rheumatism, so that he became a helpless cripple.

The fishes and reptiles then held a joint council, and arranged to haunt those human beings who tormented them with hideous dreams of serpents twining round them and of eating fish which had become decayed.

Lastly, the birds and the insects, with the smaller animals, gathered together for a similar purpose, the grub-worm presiding over the meeting. Each in turn expressed an opinion, and the consensus was against mankind. They devised and named various diseases.

When the plants, which were friendly to man, heard what had been arranged by the animals, they determined to frustrate their evil designs. Each tree, shrub and herb, down even to the grasses, agreed to furnish a remedy for some of the diseases named. When the medicine doctor was in doubt as to what treatment to apply for the relief of a patient, the spirit of the plant would suggest a fitting remedy. Thus did medicine come into being.

THE WONDERFUL KETTLE

There were once two Iroquois brothers who lived in the wilderness far from all human habitation. The elder brother went into the forest to hunt game, while the younger stayed at home and tended the hut, cooked the food, and gathered firewood.

One evening the tired hunter returned from the chase, and the younger brother took the game from him as usual and dressed it for supper. "I will smoke awhile before I eat," said the hunter, and he smoked in silence for a time. When he was tired of smoking he lay down and went to sleep.

"Strange," said the boy; "I should have thought he would want to eat first."

When the hunter awoke he found that his brother had prepared the supper and was waiting for him.

"Go to bed," said he; "I wish to be alone."

Wondering much, the boy did as he was bidden, but he could not help asking himself how his brother could possibly live if he did not eat. In the morning he observed that the hunter went away without tasting any food, and on many succeeding mornings and evenings the same thing happened.

"I must watch him at night," said the boy to himself, "for he must eat at night, since he eats at no other time."

That same evening, when the lad was told as usual to go to bed, he lay down and pretended to be sound asleep, but all the time one of his eyes was open. In this cautious fashion he watched his brother, and saw him rise from the couch and pass through a trap-door in the floor. He shortly emerged, bearing a rusty kettle, the bottom of which he scraped industriously. Filling it with water, he set it on the blazing fire. As he did so he struck it with a whip, saying at every blow: "Grow larger, my kettle!"

The obedient kettle soon became of gigantic proportions, and after setting it aside to cool the man ate its contents with evident relish.

His watchful younger brother, well content with the result of his observation, turned over and went to sleep.

When the elder had set off next morning, the boy, filled with curiosity, opened the trap-door and discovered the kettle. "I wonder what he eats," he said. There within the vessel was half a chestnut! The boy was rather surprised at this discovery, but he thought to himself how pleased his brother would be if on his return he found a meal to his taste awaiting him. When evening drew near he put the kettle on the fire, took a whip, and, hitting it repeatedly, exclaimed: "Grow larger, my kettle!"

The kettle grew larger, but to the boy's alarm it kept on growing until it filled the room, and he was obliged to get on the roof and stir it through the chimney.

"What are you doing up there?" shouted the hunter, when he came home.

"I took your kettle to get your supper ready," answered the boy.

"Alas!" cried the other, "Now I must die!"

He quickly reduced the kettle to its original proportions and put it in its place. But he still wore such a sad and serious air that his brother was filled with dismay, and prayed that he might be permitted to undo the

Each plant furnished a remedy for disease. Glycimerin from Arizona, said to be good for a cold. (Pitt Rivers Museum, Oxford.)

mischief he had wrought. When the days went past and he found that his brother no longer went out to hunt or displayed any interest in life, but grew gradually thinner and more melancholy, his distress knew no bounds.

"Let me fetch you some chestnuts," he begged earnestly. "Tell me where they may be found."

"You must travel a full day's journey," said the hunter in response to his entreaties. "You will then reach a river which is most difficult to ford. On the opposite bank there stands a lodge, and nearby a chestnut-tree. Even then your difficulties will only be beginning. The tree is guarded by a white heron, which never loses sight of it for a moment. He is employed for that purpose by the six women who live in the lodge, and with their war-clubs they slay anyone who has the temerity to approach. I beg of you, do not think of going on such a hopeless errand."

But the boy felt that even if the chance of success was even more slender, he must make the attempt for the sake of his brother, whom his thoughtlessness had brought so low.

He made a little canoe about three inches long, and set off on his journey, in the direction indicated by his brother. At the end of a day he came to the river, whose size had not been underestimated. Taking his little canoe from his pocket, he drew it out till it was of a suitable length, and launched it in the great stream. A few minutes took him to the opposite bank, and there he beheld the lodge and the chestnut tree. On his way he had managed to procure some seeds of a sort greatly liked by herons, and these he scattered before the beautiful white bird strutting round the tree. While the heron was busily engaged in picking them up, the young man seized his opportunity and gathered quantites of the chestnuts, which were lying thickly on the ground. Before his task was finished, however, the heron saw the intruder and called a loud warning to the women in the lodge, who were not slow to respond. They rushed out with their fishing-lines in their hands, and gave chase to the thief. But fear, for his brother as well as for himself, lent the youth wings, and he

A white heron guarded the tree.
(Illustration from Mark Catesby, *The Natural History of Carolina, Florida and the Bahama Islands*, 1731–43.)

Fort Clark on the Missouri in winter (right) by Karl Bodmer, from M. A. P. Wied-Neuwied, *Voyage dans l'intérieur de l'Amérique du Nord*, 1840–43.

was well out on the river in his canoe by the time the shrieking women reached the bank. The eldest threw her line and caught him, but with a sharp pull he broke it. Another line met with the same fate, and so on until all the women had thrown their lines. They could do nothing further, and were obliged to watch the retreating canoe in impotent rage.

At length the youth, having come safely through the perils of the journey, arrived home with his precious burden of chestnuts. He found his brother still alive, but so weak that he could hardly speak. A meal of the chestnuts, however, helped to revive him, and he quickly recovered.

THE CHIEF OF THE HEALING WATERS

It was winter, the snow lay thickly on the ground, and there was sorrow in the encampment, for with the cold weather a dreadful plague had visited the people. There was not one but had lost some relative, and in some cases whole families had been swept away. Among those who had been most sorely bereaved was Nekumonta, a handsome young brave, whose parents, brothers, sisters and children had died one by one before his eyes, while he was powerless to help them. Now his wife, the beautiful Shanewis, was weak and ill. The dreaded disease had laid its awful finger on her brow, and she knew that she must shortly bid her husband farewell and take her departure for the place of the dead. Already she saw her dead friends beckoning to her and inviting her to join them, but it grieved her terribly to think that she must leave her young husband in sorrow and loneliness. His despair was piteous to behold when she broke the sad news to him, but after the first outburst of grief he bore up bravely, and determined to fight the plague with all his strength.

"I must find the healing herbs which the Great Manitou has planted," said he. "Wherever they may be, I must find them."

So he made his wife comfortable on her couch, covering her with warm furs and then, embracing her gently, he set out on his difficult mission.

All day he eagerly sought in the forest for the healing herbs, but everywhere the snow lay deep, and not so much as a blade of grass was visible. When night came he crept along the frozen ground, thinking that his sense of smell might aid him in his search. Thus for three days and nights he wandered through the forest, over hills and across rivers, in a vain attempt to discover the means of curing his wife's malady.

When he met a little scurrying rabbit on the path he cried eagerly: "Tell me, where shall I find the herbs which Manitou has planted?"

But the rabbit hurried away without reply, for he knew that the herbs had not yet risen above the ground, and he was very sorry for the brave.

Nekumonta came by and by to the den of a big bear, and of this animal also he asked the same question. But the bear could give him no reply, and he was obliged to resume his weary journey. He consulted all the beasts of the forest in turn, but from none could he get any help. How could they tell him, indeed, that his search was hopeless?

On the third night he was very weak and ill, for he had tasted no food since he had first set out, and he was numbed with cold and despair. He

He launched his canoe in the great stream. Canoe manufacture. (Illustration from J. F. Lafitau, *Moeurs des Sauvages Amériquains*, 1724.)

He made a jar of clay (right). Pottery was decorated with incised designs worked into the soft clay before it was burnt to make it fire-resistant.

It really was a waterfall he heard. Montmorenci Falls near Quebec. (Illustration from the Marquis of Lorne, *Canadian Pictures, c.* 1884.)

stumbled over a withered branch hidden under the snow, and so tired was he that he lay where he fell, and immediately went to sleep. All the birds and the beasts, all the multitude of creatures that inhabit the forest came to watch over his slumbers. They remembered his kindness to them in former days, how he had never slain an animal unless he really needed it for food or clothing, how he had loved and protected the trees and the flowers. Their hearts were touched by his courageous fight for Shanewis, and they pitied his misfortunes. All that they could do to aid him they did. They cried to the Great Manitou to save his wife from the plague which held her, and the Great Spirit heard the manifold whispering and responded to their prayers.

While Nekumonta lay asleep there came to him the messenger of Manitou, and he dreamed. In his dream he saw his beautiful Shanewis, pale and thin, but as lovely as ever, and as he looked she smiled at him and sang a strange, sweet song, like the murmuring of a distant waterfall. Then the scene changed, and it really was a waterfall he heard. In musical language it called him by name, saying: "Seek us, O Nekumonta, and when you find us Shanewis shall live. We are the Healing Waters of the Great Manitou."

Nekumonta awoke with the words of the song still ringing in his ears. Starting to his feet, he looked in every direction, but there was no water to be seen, though the murmuring sound of a waterfall was distinctly audible. He fancied he could even distinguish words in it.

"Release us!" it seemed to say. "Set us free and Shanewis shall be saved!"

Nekumonta searched in vain for the waters. Then it suddenly occurred to him that they must be underground, directly under his feet. Seizing branches, stones and flints, he dug feverishly into the earth. So arduous was the task that before it was finished he was completely exhausted. But at last the hidden spring was disclosed and the waters were rippling merrily down the vale, carrying life and happiness wherever they went. The young man bathed his aching limbs in the healing stream, and in a moment he was well and strong.

Raising his hands, he gave thanks to Manitou. With eager fingers he made a jar of clay and baked it in the fire, so that he might carry life to Shanewis. As he pursued his way homeward with his treasure his despair was changed to rejoicing and he sped like the wind.

When he reached his village his companions ran to greet him. Their faces were sad and hopeless, for the plague still raged. Nekumonta directed them to the Healing Waters and inspired them with new hope. Shanewis he found on the verge of the Shadow-land, and scarcely able to murmur a farewell. But Nekumonta did not listen to her broken adieux. He forced some of the Healing Water between her parched lips, and bathed her hands and her brow till she fell into a gentle slumber. When she awoke the fever had left her. She was serene and smiling, and Nekumonta's heart was filled with happiness.

The tribe was forever rid of the dreaded plague, and the people gave to Nekomanta the title of "Chief of the Healing Waters," so that all might know that it was he who had brought them the gift of Manitou.

SAYADIO'S SISTER

Sayadio, a young Iroquois, mourned greatly for a beautiful sister who had died young. So deeply did he grieve for her that at length he resolved to seek her in the Land of Spirits. Long he sought the maiden, and many adventures did he meet with. Years passed in the search, which he was about to abandon as wholly in vain, when he encountered an old man who gave him some good advice. This venerable person also bestowed upon him a magic gourd in which he might catch and retain the spirit of his sister, should he succeed in finding her. He afterward discovered that this old man was the keeper of that part of the Spirit-land which he sought.

Delighted to have achieved so much, Sayadio continued on his way,

Mandan Bull Dance by George Catlin. Ceremonial dancing was performed by peoples all over the continent. (Illustration from *O-kee-pa: A Religious Ceremony*, 1867.)

Warrior's sash of woven trade cotton, which was worn wrapped twice around the waist. This was often referred to as an assomption sash after the area where many of them were made.

and in due time reached the Land of Souls. But to his dismay he perceived that the spirits, instead of advancing to meet him as he had expected, fled from him in terror. Greatly dejected, he approached Tarenyawago, the spirit master of ceremonies, who took compassion on him and informed him that the dead had gathered together for a great dance festival, in the same way that the Indians celebrated at certain seasons of the year. Soon the dancing commenced, and Sayadio saw the spirits floating round in a hazy measure like wreaths of mist. Among them he caught sight of his sister, and sprang forward to embrace her, but she eluded his grasp and dissolved into air.

Much cast down, the youth once more appealed to the sympathetic master of ceremonies, who gave him a magic rattle of great power, by the sound of which he might bring her back. Again the spirit-music sounded for the dance, and the dead folk thronged into the circle. Once more Sayadio saw his sister and observed that she was so wholly entranced with the music that she took no heed of his presence. Quick as thought, the young Indian dipped up the ghost with his gourd as one might net a fish, and secured the cover in spite of all the efforts of the captured soul to regain its liberty.

Retracing his steps earthward, he had no difficulty in making his way back to his native village, where he summoned his friends to come and behold his sister's resuscitation. The girl's corpse was brought from its resting-place to be reanimated with its spirit, and all was prepared for the ceremony, when a witless Indian maiden insisted on peeping into the gourd in her curiosity to see how a disembodied spirit looked. Instantly, as a bird flies forth to freedom when its cage bars are opened, the spirit of Sayadio's sister flew from the gourd before the startled youth could dash forward and shut down the cover. For a while Sayadio could not realize his loss, but at length his straining eyes revealed to him that the spirit of his sister was not within sight. In a flash he saw the ruin of his hopes, and with a broken heart he sank senseless to the earth.

THE PEACE QUEEN

A brave from the Oneida tribe of the Iroquois hunted in the forest. The red buck flashed past him, but not swifter than his arrow, for as the deer leaped he loosed its shaft and it pierced the beast's dappled hide.

The young man strode toward the carcass, knife in hand, but as he seized the horns the branches parted, and the angry face of an Onondaga warrior lowered between them.

"Leave the buck, Oneida," he commanded fiercely. "It is the spoil of my bow. I wounded the beast before you saw it."

The Oneida laughed. "My brother may have shot at the buck," he said, "but what good is that if he did not slay it?"

"The carcass is mine by right of forest law," cried the other in a rage. "Will you leave it or will you fight?"

The Oneida drew himself up and regarded the Onondaga scornfully.

"As my brother pleases," he replied. Next moment the two were locked in a life-and-death struggle.

Tall was the Onondaga, and strong as a great tree of the forest. The Oneida, lithe as a panther, fought with all the courage of youth. To and fro they swayed, till their breathing came thick and fast and the falling sweat blinded their eyes. At length they could struggle no longer, and by a mutual impulse they sprang apart.

"Ho! Onondaga," cried the younger man, "what is the point of striving over a buck? Is there no meat in the lodges of your people that they must fight for it like the mountain lion?"

"Peace, young man!" retorted the grave Onondaga. "I would not have fought for the buck had not your evil tongue roused me. But I am older than you, and I trust, wiser. Let us seek the lodge of the Peace Queen nearby, and she will award the buck to him who has the best right to it."

"It is well," said the Oneida, and side by side they sought the lodge of the Peace Queen.

Now the Five Nations in their wisdom had set apart a Seneca maiden, dwelling alone in the forest, as arbiter of quarrels between braves. The men of all tribes regarded this maiden as sacred and as apart from other women. She could not become the bride of any man.

As the Peace Queen heard the wrathful clamour of the braves outside her lodge she stepped forth, little pleased that they should thus disturb the vicinity of her dwelling.

"Peace!" she cried. "If you have a grievance, enter and state it. It is not fitting that braves should quarrel where the Peace Queen dwells."

At her words the men stood abashed. They entered the lodge and told the story of their meeting and the circumstances of the quarrel.

When they had finished the Peace Queen smiled scornfully. "So two such braves as you can quarrel over a buck?" she said. "Go, Onondaga, as the elder, and take one half of the spoil, and bear it back to your wife and children."

But the Onondaga stood his ground.

"O Queen," he said, "my wife is in the Land of Spirits, snatched from me by the Plague Demon. But my lodge does not lack food. I would marry again, and thine eyes have looked into my heart as the sun pierces the

A brave of the Iroquois hunted in the forest. (Illustration from George Catlin, *Letters on the North American Indians*, 1841.)

The Laws of the Five Nations Confederacy recited by Iroquois leaders. (Illustration from J. F. Lafitau, *Moeurs des Sauvages Amériquains*, 1724.)

darkness of the forest. Will you come to my lodge and cook my venison?"

But the Peace Queen shook her head.

"You know that the Five Nations have placed Genetaska apart to be Peace Queen," she replied firmly, "and that her vows may not be broken. Go in peace."

The Onondaga was silent.

Then spoke the Oneida. "O Peace Queen," he said, gazing steadfastly at Genetaska, whose eyes dropped before his glance, "I know that you are set apart by the Five Nations. But it is in my mind to ask you to go with me to my lodge, for I love you. What say you?"

The Peace Queen blushed and answered: "To you also I say, go in peace," but her voice was a whisper which ended in a stifled sob.

The two warriors departed, good friends now that they possessed a common sorrow. But the Peace Maiden had for ever lost her peace. For she could not forget the young Oneida brave, so tall, so strong and so gentle.

Summer darkened into autumn, and autumn whitened into winter. Innumerable warriors came to the Peace Lodge for the settlement of disputes. Outwardly Genetaska was calm and untroubled, but though she gave solace to others, her own breast could find none.

One day she sat by the lodge fire, which had burned down to a heap of cinders. She was thinking, dreaming of the young Oneida. Her thoughts went out to him as birds fly south to see the sun. Suddenly the crackling of twigs under a firm step roused her from her reverie. Quickly she glanced upward. Before her stood the youth of her dreams, pale and worn.

"Peace Queen," he said sadly, "you have brought darkness to the soul of the Oneida. No longer may he follow the hunt. The deer may sport in peace from him. No longer may he bend the bow or throw the tomahawk in content, or listen to the tale during the long nights round the campfire. You have his heart in your keeping. Say, will you not give him yours?"

Softly the Peace Queen murmured: "I will."

Hand in hand like two joyous children they sought his canoe, which bore them swiftly westward. No longer was Genetaska Peace Queen, for her vows were broken by the power of love.

The two were happy. But not so the men of the Five Nations. They were angry because the Peace Queen had broken her vows, and knew how foolish they had been to trust to the word of a young and beautiful woman. So with one voice they abolished the office of Peace Queen, and war and tumult returned once more.

War returned once more. Medal (opposite) given to Indian chiefs by the English during the American War of Independence. (British Museum.)

Obverse of the same medal (above left). Having enlisted Indian aid against the French, the English also used native forces against the rebellious white Americans.

Peint d'après nat. par Ch. Bodmer.   Imp. de Bougeard.   Gravé par R. Prévost.

CHAPTER 3

SIOUX MYTHS AND LEGENDS

I ctinike, the son of the sun-god, had offended his father and was consequently expelled from the celestial regions.

One day Ictinike encountered the Rabbit, and hailed him in a friendly manner, calling him "grandchild" and requesting him to do him a service. The Rabbit expressed his willingness to assist the god to the best of his ability, and inquired what he wished him to do.

"Oh, grandchild," said the crafty one, pointing upward to where a bird circled in the blue vault above them, "take your bow and arrow and bring down yonder bird."

The Rabbit fitted an arrow to his bow and the shaft transfixed the bird, which fell like a stone and lodged in the branches of a great tree.

"Now, grandchild," said Ictinike, "go into the tree and fetch me the game."

The Rabbit at first refused to do so, but at length he took off his clothes and climbed into the tree, where he stuck fast among the tortuous branches.

Ictinike, seeing that he could not make his way down, donned the unfortunate Rabbit's garments, and, highly amused at the animal's predicament, betook himself to the nearest village. There he encountered a chief who had two beautiful daughters, the elder of whom he married. The younger daughter, regarding this as an affront to her personal attractions, wandered off into the forest in a sulk. As she paced angrily up and down she heard someone calling to her from above, and, looking up, she beheld the unfortunate Rabbit, whose fur was adhering to the natural gum which was released from the bark of the tree. The girl cut down the tree and lit a fire near it, which melted the gum and freed the Rabbit.

The Rabbit and the chief's daughter compared notes, and discovered that the being who had tricked the one and affronted the other was the same. Together they proceeded to the chief's lodge, where the girl was laughed at because of the strange companion she had brought back with her. Suddenly an eagle appeared in the air above them. Ictinike shot at it and missed it, but the Rabbit loosed an arrow with great force and brought

Ictinike married the daughter of a Sioux chief. (Illustration from George Catlin, *Letters on the North American Indians*, 1841.)

A Sioux warrior (opposite). (Illustration by Karl Bodmer from M. A. P. Wied-Neuwied, *Voyage dans l'intérieur de l'Amérique du Nord*, 1840-43.)

Ictinike encountered the rabbit. Grey rabbit by J. J. Audubon, *The Viviparous Quadrupeds of North America*, 1846–54.

The Rabbit commanded the Indians to beat the drums. (Illustration from George Catlin, *Letters on the North American Indians*, 1841.)

it to earth. Each morning a feather of the dead bird turned into another eagle, and each morning Ictinike shot at and missed this newly created bird, which the Rabbit invariably succeeded in killing. This went on until Ictinike had quite worn out the Rabbit's clothing and was wearing a very old piece of tent skin, but the Rabbit returned to him the garments he had been forced to don when Ictinike had stolen his. Then the Rabbit commanded the Indians to beat the drums, and each time they were beaten Ictinike jumped so high that every bone in his body was shaken. At length, after a more than usually loud series of beats, he leapt to such a height that when he came down it was found that the fall had broken his neck. The Rabbit was avenged.

Ictinike and the Buzzard

One day Ictinike, footsore and weary, encountered a buzzard. He asked the bird to oblige him by carrying him on its back part of the way. The crafty buzzard immediately consented and, seating Ictinike between its wings, flew off with him.

They had not gone far when they passed above a hollow tree, and Ictinike began to shift uneasily in his seat as he observed the buzzard hovering over it. He requested the bird to fly on, but for answer it cast him headlong into the tree trunk, where he found himself a prisoner. For a long time he lay there in pain and wretchedness, until at last a large hunting-party struck camp at the spot. Ictinike chanced to be wearing some racoon skins, and he thrust the tails of these through the cracks in the tree. Three women who were standing near imagined that a number of racoons had become imprisoned in the hollow trunk, and they made a large hole

in it for the purpose of capturing the animals. Ictinike at once emerged, whereupon the women fled. Ictinike lay on the ground pretending to be dead, and as he was covered with the racoon-skins the birds of prey—the eagle, the rook and the magpie—came to devour him. While they pecked at him the buzzard made his appearance for the purpose of joining in the feast, but Ictinike, rising up, tore the feathers from its scalp. That is why the buzzard has no feathers on its head to this day.

Ictinike goes visiting

In the course of time, Ictinike married and dwelt in a lodge of his own. One day he told his wife that he intended to visit her grandfather, the Beaver. On arriving at the Beaver's lodge he found that his grandfather-in-law and his family had been without food for a long time, and were slowly dying of starvation. Ashamed at having no food to pleace before their guest, one of the young beavers offered himself up to provide a meal for Ictinike, and was duly cooked and served to the visitor. Before Ictinike partook of the dish, however, the Beaver earnestly requested him not to break any of the bones of his son, but unwittingly Ictinike split one of the toe-bones. Having finished his repast, he lay down to rest, and the Beaver gathered the bones and put them in a skin. This he plunged into the river that flowed beside his lodge, and in a moment the young beaver emerged from the water alive.

"How do you feel, my son?" asked the Beaver.

Sioux Camp Scene by A. J. Miller. Traditionally the Sioux used buffalo hide for their tepees. (Kennedy Galleries, New York.)

"Alas! father," replied the young beaver, "one of my toes is broken."

From that time on every beaver has had one toe—that next to the little one—which looks as if it had been split by biting.

Shortly after, Ictinike took his leave of the Beavers and pretended to forget his tobacco-pouch, which he left behind. The Beaver told one of his young ones to run after him with the pouch, but, being aware of Ictinike's treacherous character, he advised his offspring to throw it to the god while still some distance away. The young beaver accordingly took the pouch and hurred after Ictinike, and, obeying his father's instruction, was about to throw it to him from a considerable distance when Ictinike called to him: "Come closer, come closer."

The young beaver obeyed, and as Ictinike took the pouch from him he said: "Tell your father that he must visit me."

When the young beaver arrived home he told his father what had passed, and the Beaver showed signs of great annoyance.

"I knew he would say that," he growled, "and that is why I did not want you to go near him."

But the Beaver could not refuse the invitation, and in due course returned the visit. Ictinike, wishing to pay him a compliment, was about to kill one of his own children to feed the Beaver, and was slapping it to make it cry in order to work himself into a passion sufficiently murderous to enable him to take its life, when the Beaver spoke to him sharply and told him that such a sacrifice was unnecessary. Going down to the nearby stream, the Beaver found a young beaver by the water, which was brought up to the lodge, killed and cooked and duly eaten.

On another occasion Ictinike announced to his wife his intention of calling upon her grandfather the Muskrat. At the Muskrat's lodge he met with the same tale of starvation as at the home of the Beaver, but the Muskrat told his wife to fetch some water, put it in the kettle, and hang the kettle over the fire. When the water was boiling the Muskrat upset the kettle, which was found to be full of wild rice, upon which Ictinike feasted. As before, he left his tobacco-pouch with his host, and the Muskrat sent one of his children after him with it. An invitation for the Muskrat to visit him resulted, and the call was duly paid. Ictinike,

Ictinike left his tobacco-pouch behind. Although the arrival of the horse turned many Plains tribes into nomads, they continued to cultivate tobacco. (Pitt Rivers Museum, Oxford.)

Ictinike visited the Muskrat (right). Muskrat by J. J. Audubon, *The Viviparous Quadrupeds of North America*, 1846–54.

wishing to display his magical powers, requested his wife to hang a kettle of water over the fire, but to his chagrin, when the water was boiled and the kettle upset, instead of wild rice only water poured out. Thereupon the Muskrat had the kettle refilled, and produced an abundance of rice, much to Ictinike's annoyance.

Ictinike then called upon his wife's grandfather the Kingfisher, who, to provide him with food, dived into the river and brought up fish. Ictinike extended a similar invitation to him, and the visit was duly paid. Desiring to be even with his late host, the god dived into the river in search of fish. He soon found himself in difficulties, however, and if it had not been for the Kingfisher he would most assuredly have been drowned.

Lastly, Ictinike went to visit his wife's grandfather the Flying Squirrel. The Squirrel climbed to the top of his lodge and brought down a quantity of excellent black walnuts, which Ictinike ate. When he departed from the Squirrel's house he purposely left one of his gloves, which a small squirrel brought after him, and he sent an invitation by this messenger for the Squirrel to visit him in turn. Wishing to show his cleverness, Ictinike scrambled to the top of his lodge, but instead of finding any black walnuts there, he fell and severely injured himself. Thus his boldness was punished for the fourth time.

The Flying Squirrel climbed to the top of his lodge. (Illustration from Mark Catesby, *The Natural History of Carolina, Florida and the Bahama islands*, 1731–43.)

THE MEN-SERPENTS

Twenty warriors who had been on the war-path were returning homeward worn out and hungry, and as they went they scattered in search of game to sustain them on their way.

Suddenly one of the braves, placing his ear to the ground, declared that he could hear a herd of buffaloes approaching.

The band was greatly cheered by this news and the plans made by the chief to intercept the animals were quickly carried into effect.

Nearer and nearer came the supposed herd. The chief lay very still, ready to shoot when it came within range. Suddenly he saw, to his horror, that what approached them was a huge snake with a rattle as large as a

Sioux war club dating from *c.* 1880, made of stone, wood and leather for ceremonial use. (Joslyn Art Museum, Omaha, Nebraska.)

A huge snake with a rattle as large as a man's head. Rattlesnakes are unique to the Americas and found from Canada southwards.

The foothills of the Rocky Mountains mark the western boundary of the territory inhabited by the Sioux.

Red Indian Horsemanship (opposite) by George Catlin. The Spanish introduced the horse in the mid sixteenth century and thus altered native ways of life entirely. (Smithsonian Institution, Washington, D.C.)

man's head. Though almost paralysed with surprise and terror, he managed to shoot the monster and kill it. He called up his men, who were not a little afraid of the gigantic creature even though it was dead, and for a long time they debated what they should do with the carcass.

At length hunger conquered their scruples and made them decide to cook and eat it. To their surprise, they found the meat as savoury as that of a buffalo, which it much resembled. Everyone had some of the meat, with the exception of one boy, who persisted in refusing it however much they pressed him to eat. When the warriors had finished their meal they lay down beside the camp-fire and fell asleep.

Later in the night the chief awoke and was horrified to find that his companions had turned to snakes, and that he himself was already half snake, half man. Hastily he gathered together his transformed warriors, and they saw that the boy who had not eaten of the reptile had retained his own human form. The lad, fearing that the serpents might attack him, began to weep, but the snake-warriors treated him very kindly, giving him their charms and all they possessed.

At their request he put them into a large robe and carried them to the summit of a high hill, where he set them down under the trees.

"You must return to our lodges," they told him, "and in the summer we will visit our kindred. When that time comes, you must make sure that our wives and children come out to greet us."

The boy carried the news to his village, and there was much weeping and lamentation when the friends of the warriors heard of their fate. In the summer the snakes came and sat in a group outside the village, and all the people crowded round them, loudly venting their grief. The horses which had belonged to the snakes were brought out to them, as well as their moccasins, leggings, whips and saddles.

"Do not be afraid of them," said the boy to the assembled people. "Do not flee from them, lest something happen to you also." So they let the snakes creep over them, and no harm came to them.

So the men-serpents stayed in their village for the summer, but in the winter they vanished altogether, along with their horses and other possessions, and the people never saw them again.

THE THREE TESTS

A woman of remarkable grace and attractiveness (above) drew suitors from far and wide. (Illustration from R. I. Dodge, *The Hunting Grounds of the Great West*, 1877.)

There lived in a certain village a woman of remarkable grace and attractiveness. The fame of her beauty drew suitors from far and near, eager to display their prowess and win the love of this imperious creature—for, besides being beautiful, she was extremely hard to please and set such difficult tests for her loves that no-one had yet been able to satisfy her.

A certain young man, who lived a considerable distance away, had heard of her charms, and made up his mind to win her. The difficulty of the task did not daunt him and, full of hope, he set out on his mission.

As he travelled towards the woman's village he came to a very high hill, and on the summit he saw a man rising and sitting down at short intervals. When the prospective suitor drew nearer he observed that the man was fastening large stones to his ankles. The youth approached him,

He came to a very high hill. Jasper National Park, Rocky Mountains, West Alberta, marks the edge of the area occupied by the Plains Indians.

saying: "Why do you tie those great stones to your ankles?"

"Oh," replied the other, "I wish to chase buffaloes, and yet whenever I do so I go beyond them, so I am tying stones to my ankles that I may not run so fast."

"My friend," said the suitor, "you can run some other time. In the meantime I am without a companion. Come with me."

The Swift One agreed, and they walked on their way together. Before they had gone very far they saw two large lakes. By the side of one of them sat a man, who frequently bowed his head to the water and drank. Surprised that his thirst was not quenched, they said to him: "Why do you sit there drinking from the lake?"

"I can never get enough water. When I have finished this lake I shall start on the other."

"My friend," said the suitor, "do not trouble to drink it just now. Come and join us."

The Thirsty One agreed, and the three comrades journeyed on. When they had gone a little farther they noticed a man walking along with his face lifted to the sky. Curious to know why he acted thus they addressed him.

"Why do you walk with your eyes turned skyward?" said they.

"I have shot an arrow," he said, "and I am waiting for it to reappear."

"Never mind your arrow," said the suitor. "Come with us."

"I will come," said the Skilful Archer.

As the four companions journeyed through a forest they beheld a strange sight. A man was lying with his ear to the ground, and if he lifted his head for a moment he bowed it again, listening intently. The four approached him, saying: "Friend, for what do you listen so earnestly?"

"I am listening," said he, "to the plants growing. This forest is full of plants, and I am listening to their breathing."

"You can listen when the occasion arises," they told him. "Come and join us."

He agreed, and so they travelled to the beautiful maiden's village.

When they had reached their destination they were quickly surrounded by the villagers, who displayed much curiosity as to who their visitors were and what object they had in coming so far. When they heard that one of the strangers desired to marry the village beauty they shook their heads over him. Did he not know the difficulties in the way? Finding that he would not be turned from his purpose, they led him to a huge rock which overshadowed the village, and described the first test he would be required to meet.

"If you wish to win the maiden," they said, "you must first of all push away that great stone. It is keeping the sunlight from us."

"Alas!" said the youth. "It is impossible."

"Not so," said his companion of the swift foot. "Nothing could be more easy."

Saying this, he leaned his shoulder against the rock, and with a mighty crash, it fell from its place. From the breaking up of it came the rocks and stones that are scattered over all the world.

The second test was of a different nature. The people brought the strangers a large quantity of food and water, and bade them eat and drink. Being very hungry, they succeeded in disposing of the food, but the suitor sorrowfully regarded the great kettles of water.

"Impossible!" said he. "Who can drink up that?"

"I can," said the Thirsty One, and in a twinkling he had drunk it all.

The people were amazed at the prowess of the visitors. However, they said: "There is still another test," and they brought out a woman who was a very swift runner, so swift that no-one had ever outstripped her in a race.

The people brought them water. Drinking cup from Perry County, Missouri. (Collection of the Chicago Academy of Sciences.)

They travelled to the village. A typical Piegan encampment of the Plains from Edward Curtis, *The North American Indian*, 1907–30.

"You must run a race with this woman," said they. "If you win you shall have the hand of the maiden you have come to seek."

Naturally the suitor chose the Swift One for this test. When the runners started the people hailed them as fairly matched, for they raced together till they were out of sight.

When they reached the turning-point the woman said: "Come, let us rest for a little."

The man agreed, but no sooner had he sat down than he fell asleep. The woman seized her opportunity. Making sure that her rival was sleeping soundly, she set off for the village, running as hard as she could.

Meanwhile the four comrades were anxiously awaiting the return of the competitors, and great was their disappointment when the woman came in sight while there was yet no sign of their champion.

The man who could hear the plants growing bent his ear to the ground.

"He is asleep," said he. "I can hear him snoring."

The Skilful Archer came forward, and as he bit the point off an arrow he said: "I will soon wake him."

He shot an arrow from the bowstring with such a wonderful aim that it wounded the sleeper's nose, and roused him from his slumbers. The runner started to his feet and looked round for the woman. She was gone. Knowing that he had been tricked, the Swift One put all his energy into an effort to overtake her. She was within a few yards of the winning-post when he passed her. It was a narrow margin, but nevertheless the Swift One had won the race for his comrade.

The youth was then married to the damsel, whom he found to be all that her admirers had claimed, and more.

The Skilful Archer shot an arrow.
(Illustration by Karl Bodmer from
M. A. P. Wied-Neuwied, *Voyage dans
l'intérieur de l'Amérique du Nord*,
1840–43.)

THE SNAKE-OGRE

One day a young brave, feeling at variance with the world in general, and wishing to rid himself of the mood, left the lodges of his people and journeyed into the forest. By and by he came to an open space, in the centre of which was a high hill. Thinking he would climb to the top and observe the land, he directed his footsteps thither, and as he went he observed a man coming in the opposite direction and making for the same spot. The two met on the summit, and stood for a few moments silently regarding each other. The stranger was the first to speak, gravely inviting the young brave to accompany him to his lodge and sup with him. The other accepted the invitation, and they proceeded in the direction the stranger indicated.

On approaching the lodge the youth saw with some surprise that there was a large heap of bones in front of the door. Inside sat a very old woman tending a pot. When the young man learned that the feast was to be a cannibal one, however, he declined to partake of it. The woman thereupon boiled some corn for him, and while doing so she told him that his host was nothing less than a snake-man, a sort of ogre who killed and ate human beings. Because the brave was young and very handsome the old woman took pity on him, bemoaning the fate that would surely befall him

He came to an open space. Desert scrub and eroded rock forms in the region known as the Badlands, South Dakota.

unless he could succeed in escaping from the wiles of the snake-man.

"Listen," said she: "I will tell you what to do. Here are some moccasins. When the morning comes put them on your feet, take one step, and you will find yourself on that headland you see in the distance. Give this paper to the man you will meet there, and he will direct you further. But remember that however far you may go, in the evening the Snake will overtake you. When you have finished with the moccasins take them off, place them on the ground facing this way, and they will return."

"Is that all?" said the youth.

"No," she replied. "Before you go you must kill me and put a robe over my bones."

The young brave proceeded to carry these instructions into effect. First of all he killed the old woman and disposed of her remains in accordance with her bidding. In the morning he put on the magic moccasins which she had provided for him, and with one great step he reached the distant headland. Here he met an old man, who took the paper from him and then, giving him another pair of moccasins, directed him to a far-off point where he was to deliver another piece of paper to a man who would await him there. Turning the first moccasins homeward, the young brave put the second pair to use, and took another gigantic step. Arriving at the second stage of his journey from the Snake's lodge, he found it a repetition of the first. He was directed to another distant spot, and from that to yet another. But when he delivered his message for the fourth time he was treated somewhat differently.

A place where the river widened. Junction of Yellowstone and Missouri rivers. (Illustration by Karl Bodmer from M. A. P. Wied-Neuwied, *Voyage dans l'intérieur de l'Amérique du Nord,* 1840–43.)

He saw a very large fish. Arctic grayling, after painting by S. A. Kilbourne, from *Game Fish of the United States,* 1878–80.

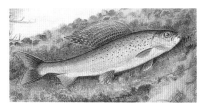

"Down there in the hollow," said the recipient of the paper, "there is a stream. Go towards it, and walk straight on, but do not look at the water."

The youth did as he was bidden, and shortly found himself on the opposite bank of the stream.

He journeyed up the creek, and as evening fell he came upon a place where the river widened to a lake. Skirting its shores, he suddenly found himself face to face with the Snake. Only then did he remember the words of the old woman, who had warned him that in the evening the Snake would overtake him. So he turned himself into a little fish with red fins, lazily moving in the lake.

The Snake, high on the bank, saw the little creature, and cried: "Little Fish! have you seen the person I am looking for? If a bird had flown over the lake you must have seen it, the water is so still, so surely you have seen the man I am seeking?"

"Not so," replied the little fish, "I have seen no-one. But if he passes this way I will tell you."

So the Snake continued downstream, and as he went there was a little grey toad right in his path.

"Little Toad," said he, "have you seen the man I am seeking? Even if only a shadow were here you must have seen it."

"Yes," said the little toad, "I have seen him, but cannot tell you which way he has gone."

The Snake doubled back and came on his trail. Seeing a very large fish in the shallow water, he said "Have you seen the man I am looking for?"

"That is he with whom you have just been talking," said the fish, and the Snake turned homeward. Meeting a muskrat he stopped.

"Have you seen the person I am looking for?" he said. Then, having his suspicions aroused, he added craftily: "I think that you are he."

But the muskrat began a bitter complaint.

"Just now," said he, "the person you seek passed over my lodge and broke it."

So the Snake passed on, and encountered a red-breasted turtle.

He repeated his query, and the turtle told him that the object of his search would be met with farther on.

"But beware," he added, "for if you do not recognize him he will kill you."

Following the stream, the Snake came upon a large green frog floating in shallow water.

"I have been seeking a person since morning," he said. "I think that you are he."

The frog allayed his suspicions, saying: "You will meet him farther down the stream."

The Snake next found a large turtle floating among the green scum on a lake. Getting on the turtle's back, he said "You must be the person I seek," and his head rose higher and higher as he prepared to strike.

"I am not," replied the turtle. "The next person you meet will be he. But beware, for if you do not recognize him he will kill you."

When he had gone a little farther down the Snake attempted to cross the stream. In the middle was an eddy. Crafty as he was, the Snake failed to recognize his enemy, and the eddy drew him down into the water and drowned him. So the youth succeeded in slaying the Snake who had sought throughout the day to kill him.

The Story of the Salmon

A certain chief who had a very beautiful daughter was unwilling to part with her, but knowing that the time must come when she would marry, he arranged a contest for her suitors in which the feat was to break a pair of elk's antlers hung in the centre of the lodge.

He came upon a large green frog. (Illustration from Mark Catesby, *The Natural History of Carolina, Florida and the Bahama islands*, 1731–43.)

Next he found a large turtle. (Illustration from Mark Catesby, *The Natural History of Carolina, Florida and the Bahama islands*, 1731–43.)

"Whoever manages to break these antlers," the old chief declared, "shall be entitled to have the hand of my daughter."

The quadrupeds came first—the Squirrel, Otter, Beaver, Wolf, Bear and Panther; but all their strength and skill was not enough to break the antlers. Next came the Birds, but their efforts also were to no avail. The only creature left who had not attempted the feat was a feeble thing covered with sores whom the mischievous Blue Jay derisively summoned to perform the task. After repeated taunts from the tricky bird, the creature rose, shook itself, and became whole and clean and very good to look upon, and the assembled company saw that it was the Salmon. He grasped the elk's antlers and easily broke them in five pieces. Then, claiming his prize, the chief's daughter, he led her away.

Before they had gone very far the people said: "Let us go and take the chief's daughter back," and they set off in pursuit of the pair along the sea-shore.

When Salmon saw what was happening he created a bay between himself and his pursuers. The people at length reached the point of the bay on which Salmon stood, but he made another bay, and when they looked they could see him on the far-off point of that one. So the chase went on, till Salmon grew tired of exercising his magic powers.

Coyote and Badger, who were ahead of the others, decided to shoot at Salmon. The arrow hit him in the neck and killed him instantly. When

Sioux chiefs indicated their standing by the length and splendour of their feather warbonnets. (Illustration from Edward Curtis, *The North American Indian*, 1907–30.)

The assembled company saw that it was the Salmon. Spawning Sockeye salmon from Scotch Creek, British Columbia.

the rest of the band came up they gave the chief's daughter to the Wolves, and she became the wife of one of them.

In due time the people returned to their village, and the Crow, who was Salmon's aunt, learned of his death. She hastened away to the spot where he had been killed to seek for his remains, but all she could find was one salmon's egg, which she hid in a hole in the river-bank. Next day she found that the egg was much larger; on the third day it was a small trout, and so it grew till it became a full-grown salmon, and at length a handsome youth.

Leading young Salmon to a mountain pool, his grand-aunt said: "Bathe there, that you may see spirits."

One day Salmon said: "I am tired of seeing spirits. Let me go away."

The old Crow thereupon told him of his father's death at the hands of Badger and Coyote.

"They have taken your father's bow," she said.

The Salmon shot an arrow toward the forest and the forest caught fire. He shot an arrow toward the prairie, and it also caught fire.

"Truly," muttered the old Crow, "you have seen spirits."

Having made up his mind to get his father's bow, Salmon journeyed to the lodge where Coyote and Badger lived. He found the door shut and the creatures with their faces blackened, pretending to lament the death of old Salmon. However, he was not deceived by their tricks, but boldly entered and demanded his father's bow. Four times they gave him other bows, which broke when he drew them. The fifth time it was really his father's bow which he received. Taking Coyote and Badger outside, he knocked them together and killed them.

As he travelled across the prairie, Salmon stumbled on the habitation of the Wolves and on entering the lodge he encountered his father's wife, who bade him hide before the monsters returned. By means of strategy he got the better of them, shot them all and sailed away in a little boat with the woman. Out on the water he fell into a deep sleep, and slept so long that at last his companion ventured to wake him. Very angry at

being roused, he turned her into a pigeon and cast her out of the boat, while he himself, in his shape of a salmon, swam back to the shore.

Near the edge of the water was a lodge, where dwelt five beautiful sisters. Salmon sat on the shore at a little distance, and took the form of an aged man covered with sores. When the eldest sister came down to speak to him he bade her carry him on her back to the lodge, but so loathsome a creature was he that she beat a hasty retreat. The second sister did likewise, and the third and the fourth. But the youngest sister agreed to carry him to the lodge, where he became again a young and handsome brave. He married all the sisters, but the youngest was his head-wife and his favourite.

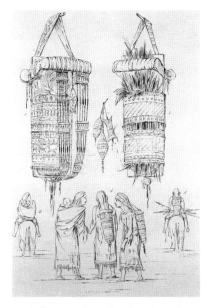

A Sioux cradle and modes of carrying children. (Illustration from George Catlin, *Letters on the North American Indians*, 1841.)

The two men painted their bodies. Crow Indians by Karl Bodmer. (Illustration from M. A. P. Wied-Nieuwied, *Voyage dans l'intérieur de l'Amérique du Nord*, 1840–43.)

THE DROWNED CHILD

On the banks of a river there lived a worthy couple with their only son, a little child whom they loved dearly. One day the boy wandered away from the lodge and fell into the water, and no one was near enough to rescue him. Great was the distress of the parents when the news reached them, and all his relatives were loud in their lamentations, for the child had been a favourite with everybody. The father especially showed signs of the deepest grief, and refused to enter his lodge till he should recover the boy. All night he lay outside on the bare ground, his cheek pillowed on his hand. Suddenly he heard a faint sound, far under the earth. He listened intently: it was the crying of his lost child! Hastily he gathered all his relatives round him, told them what he had heard, and piteously besought them to dig into the earth and bring back his son. This task they hesitated to undertake, but they willingly collected horses and goods in abundance, to be given to anyone who would venture to do so.

Two men came forward who claimed to possess supernatural powers, and to them was entrusted the work of finding the child. The grateful father gave them a pipe filled with tobacco, and promised them all his possessions if their mission should succeed. The two gifted men painted their bodies, one making himself quite black, the other yellow. Going to the neighbouring river, they plunged into its depths, and soon arrived at the abode of the Water-god. This being and his wife, having no children of their own, had adopted the Indian's little son who was supposed to have been drowned. The two men, seeing him alive and well, were pleased to think that their task was as good as accomplished.

"The father has sent for his son," they said. "He has commanded us to bring him back. We dare not return without him."

"You are too late," responded the Water-god. "Had you come before he had eaten of my food he might safely have returned with you. But he wished to eat, and he has eaten, and now, alas! he would die if he were taken out of the water."

Sorrowfully the men rose to the surface and carried the tidings to the father.

"Alas!" they said, "he has eaten in the palace of the Water-god. He will die if we bring him home."

The winter camp of the Sioux (opposite) was made in forested valleys, protected from the winds of the plains. (Illustration from Edward Curtis, *The North American Indian*, 1907–30.)

Nevertheless the father persisted in his desire to see the child again.

"I must see him," he said, and the two men prepared for a second journey, saying: "If you get him back, the Water-god will require a white dog in payment."

The Indian promised to supply the dog. The two men painted themselves again, the one black, the other yellow. Once more they dived through the clear water to the palace of the god.

"The father must have his child," they said. "This time we dare not return without him."

So the deity gave up the little boy, who was placed in his father's arms, dead. At the sight the grief of his relatives burst out afresh. However, they did not forget to cast a white dog into the river, nor to pay the men lavishly, as they had promised.

Later the parents lost a daughter in the same manner, but as she had eaten nothing of the food offered her under the water she was brought back alive, on payment of a tribute to the Water-god of four white dogs.

Dakota woman and Assinboin girl. (Illustration by Karl Bodmer from M. A. P. Wied-Neuwied, *Voyage dans l'intérieur de l'Amérique du Nord,* 1840–43.)

A song of thanksgiving to the deity. A Sioux supplicant offers a prayer to the Mystery. (Illustration from Edward Curtis, *The North American Indian,* 1907–30.)

THE SNAKE-WIFE

A certain chief advised his son to travel. Idling, he pointed out, was not the way to qualify for chieftainship.

"When I was your age," said he, "I did not sit still. There was hard work to be done. And now look at me: I have become a great chief."

"I will go hunting, father," said the youth. So his father furnished him with good clothing and had a horse saddled for him.

The young man went off on his expedition and by and by fell in with some elk. Shooting at the largest beast, he wounded it slightly, and as it dashed away he spurred his horse after it. In this manner they covered a considerable distance, till at length the hunter, worn out with thirst and fatigue, reined in his steed and dismounted. He wandered about in search of water till he was almost spent, but after a time he came upon a spring and immediately improvised a song of thanksgiving to the deity, Wakanda, who had permitted him to find it. His rejoicing was somewhat premature, however, for when he approached the spring a snake started up from it.

The youth was badly scared, and retreated to a safe distance without drinking. It seemed as though he must die of thirst after all. Venturing to look back after a time, he saw that the snake had disappeared, and very cautiously he returned. Again the snake darted from the water, and the thirsty hunter was forced to flee. A third return to the spring had no happier results, but when his thirst drove him to a fourth attempt the youth found, instead of a snake, a very beautiful woman. She offered him a drink in a small cup, which she replenished as often as he emptied it. So struck was he by her grace and beauty that he promptly fell in love with her. When it was time for him to return home she gave him a ring, saying: "When you sit down to eat, place this ring on a seat and say, 'Come, let us eat,' and I will come to you."

Having bidden her farewell, the young man turned his steps homeward,

and when he was once more among his kinsfolk he asked for food to be placed before him. "Make haste," said he, "for I am very hungry."

Quickly they obeyed him, and set down a variety of dishes. When he was alone the youth drew the ring from his finger and laid it on a seat. "Come," he said, "let us eat."

Immediately the Snake-woman appeared and joined him at his meal. When she had eaten she vanished as mysteriously as she had come, and the disconsolate husband (for the youth had married her) went out of the lodge to seek her. Thinking she might be among the women of the village, he said to his father "Let the women dance before me."

An old man was sent to gather the women together, but not one of them so much as resembled the Snake-woman.

Again the youth sat down to eat, and repeated the formula which his wife had described to him. She ate with him as before, and vanished when the meal was over.

"Father," said the young man, "let the very young women dance before me."

But the Snake-woman was not found among them either.

Another fleeting visit from his wife encouraged the chief's son to make yet another attempt to find her in the community.

"Let the young girls dance," he said. Still the mysterious Snake-woman was not found.

One day a girl overheard voices in the youth's lodge, and, peering in, saw a beautiful woman sharing his meal. She told the news to the chief, and it soon became known that the chief's son was married to a stranger.

The young man fell in with some elk. The Moose Chase by George de Forest Brusch (b. 1855). (National Museum of American Art, Smithsonia.)

Silver and turquoise ring of the type made by the Navajo after about 1880. Such decorative items reached the Plains Indians via extensive trade networks across the continent.

The youth, however, wished to marry a woman of his own tribe, but the maiden's father, having heard that the young man was already married, told his daughter that she was only being made fun of.

So the girl had nothing more to do with her wooer, who turned for consolation to his ring. He caused food to be brought, then placed the ring on a seat.

"Come," he said, "let us eat."

There was no response; the Snake-woman would not appear.

The youth was greatly disappointed, and made up his mind to go in search of his wife.

"I am going hunting," said he, and again his father gave him good clothes and saddled a horse for him.

When he reached the spot where the Snake-woman had first met him, he found her trail leading up to the spring, and beyond it on the other side. Still following the trail, he saw before him a very dilapidated lodge, at the door of which sat an old man in rags. The youth felt very sorry for the tattered old fellow, and gave him his fine clothes, in exchange for which he received the other's rags.

"You think you are doing me a good turn," said the old man, "but it is I who am going to do you one. The woman you seek has gone over the Great Water. When you get to the other shore, talk with the people you shall meet there, and if they do not obey you, send them away."

In addition to the tattered garments, the old man gave him a hat, a sword and a lame old horse.

At the edge of the Great Water the youth prepared to cross, while his companion seated himself on the shore, closed his eyes and recited a spell. In a moment the young man found himself on the opposite shore. Here he found a lodge inhabited by two aged Thunder-men, who were apparently given to eating human beings. The young stranger made the discovery that his hat rendered him invisible, and he was able to move unseen among the creatures. Taking off his hat for a moment, he took the pipe from the mouth of a Thunder-man and pressed it against the latter's hand.

"Oh," cried the Thunder-man, "I am burnt!"

But the youth had clapped on his hat and disappeared.

"It is not well," said the Thunder-man gravely. "A stranger has been here and we have let him escape. When our brother returns he will not believe us if we tell him the man has vanished."

Shortly after this another Thunder-man entered with the body of a man he had killed. When the brothers told him their story he was quite sceptical.

"If I had been here," said he, "I would not have let him escape."

As he spoke the youth snatched his pipe from him and pressed it against the back of his hand.

"Oh," said the Thunder-man, "I am burnt!"

"It was not I," said one brother.

"It was not I," said the other.

"It was I," said the youth, pulling off his hat and appearing among them. "What were you talking about among yourselves? Here I am. Do as you said."

But the Thunder-men were afraid.

"Let the women dance before me." Mandan women dancing. (Illustration by Karl Bodmer from M. A. P. Wied-Neuwied, *Voyage dans l'intérieur de l'Amérique du Nord.* 1840–43.)

The youth prepared to cross the Great Water, while his companion recited a spell. Banff National Park, Rocky Mountains, West Alberta.

"We were not speaking," they said, and the youth put on his hat and vanished.

"What will our brother say," cried the three in dismay, "when he hears that a man has been here and we have not killed him? Our brother will surely hate us."

In a few minutes another Thunder-man came into the lodge, carrying the body of a child. He was very angry when he heard that they had let a man escape.

The youth repeated his trick on the newcomer—appeared for a moment, then vanished again. The fifth and last of the brothers was also deceived in the same manner.

Seeing that the monsters were now thoroughly frightened, the young man took off his magic hat and talked with them.

"You do wrong," said he, "to eat men like this. You should eat buffaloes, not men. I am going away. When I come back I will visit you, and if you are eating buffaloes you shall remain, but if you are eating men I shall send you away."

The Thunder-men promised they would eat only buffaloes in future, and the young man went on his way to seek for the Snake-woman. When at last he came to the village where she lived, he found she had married a man from another tribe, and in a great rage he swung the sword the magician had given him and killed her, and her husband and the whole village, after which he returned the way he had come. When he reached the lodge of the Thunder-men he saw that they had not kept their promise to eat only buffaloes.

"I am going to send you above," he said. "Hitherto you have destroyed men, but when I have sent you away you shall give them cooling rain to keep them alive."

So he sent them above, where they became the thunder-clouds.

Proceeding on his journey, he again crossed the Great Water with a

Beaded Sioux warshirt made of deerskin with a fringe of human hair. Such garments were often referred to as "scalp shirts" although the hair was generally given to the wearer in ceremony.

His relatives had perished (left). Funeral scaffold of a Sioux chief by Karl Bodmer from M. A. P. Wied-Neuwied, *Voyage dans l'intérieur de l'Amérique du Nord*, 1840–43.

single stride, and related to the old wizard all that he had been doing.

"I have sent the Thunder-men above, because they would not stop eating men. Have I done well?"

"Very well."

"I have killed the whole village where the Snake-woman was, because she had taken another husband. Have I done well?"

"Very well. It was for that I gave you the sword."

The youth returned to his father, and married a very beautiful woman from his own village.

The youth returned to his father and married a beautiful woman. A Mandan warrior, chief and young woman by George Catlin. (Illustration from *O-kee-pa: A Religious Ceremony,* 1867.)

"Put the feather on your head." The number of feathers worn and their positioning denoted the rank of the wearer. (Illustration from Edward Curtis, *The North American Indian,* 1907-30.)

WHITE FEATHER THE GIANT-KILLER

There once dwelt in the heart of a great forest an old man and his grandchild. So far as he could remember, the boy had never seen any human being but his grandfather, and though he frequently questioned the latter on the subject of his relatives he could elicit no information from him. The truth was that they had perished at the hands of six great giants. The nation to which the boy belonged had wagered their children against those of the giants that they would beat the latter in a race. Unfortunately the giants won, the children of the rash Indians were forfeited, and all were killed, with the exception of little Chácopee, whose grandfather had taken charge of him. The child learned to hunt and fish, and seemed quite contented and happy.

One day the boy wandered away to the edge of a prairie, where he found traces of an encampment. Returning, he told his grandfather of the ashes and tent-poles he had seen, and asked for an explanation. Had his grandfather set them there? The old man responded brusquely that there were no ashes or tentpoles: he had merely imagined them. The boy was sorely puzzled, but he let the matter drop, and next day he followed a different path. Quite suddenly he heard a voice addressing him as "Wearer of the White Feather." Now there had been a tradition in his tribe that a mighty man would arise among them wearing a white feather and performing astonishing feats of bravery. But Chácopee as yet knew nothing of this, so he could only look about him in a startled way. Close by him stood a man, which fact was in itself sufficiently astonishing to the boy, who had never seen any one but his grandfather, but to his further bewilderment, he perceived that the man was made of wood from the breast downward, only the head being of flesh.

"You do not wear the white feather yet," the curious stranger resumed, "but you will, by and by. Go home and sleep. You will dream of a pipe, a sack and a large white feather. When you wake you will see these things by your side. Put the feather on your head and you will become a very great warrior. If you want proof, smoke the pipe and you will see the smoke turn into pigeons."

He then proceeded to tell him who his parents were and of the manner in which they had perished, and bade him avenge their death on the giants. To aid him in the accomplishment of this feat he gave him a magic vine which would be invisible to the giants, and with which he would therefore be able to trip them up when they ran a race with him.

Chácopee returned home, and everything happened as the Man of Wood had predicted. The old grandfather was greatly surprised to see a flock of pigeons issuing from the lodge, from which Chácopee also shortly emerged, wearing on his head a white feather. Remembering the prophecy, the old man wept to think that he might lose his grandchild.

Next morning Chácopee set off in search of the giants, whom he found in a very large lodge in the centre of the forest. The giants had learned of his approach from the "little spirits who carry the news."

Among themselves they mocked and scoffed at him, but outwardly they greeted him with much civility. He was in no way deceived, however, as to their true feelings.

Without loss of time they arranged a race between Chácopee and the youngest giant, the winner of which was to cut off the head of the other. Chácopee won, with the help of his magic vine, and killed his opponent. Next morning he appeared again, and decapitated another of his foes. This happened on five mornings. On the sixth he set out as usual, but was met by the Man of Wood, who informed him that on his way to the giants' lodge he would encounter the most beautiful woman in the world.

"Pay no attention to her," he said earnestly. "She is there for your destruction. When you see her, turn yourself into an elk, and you will be safe from her wiles."

Chácopee proceeded on his way, and sure enough, before long he met the most beautiful woman in the world. Mindful of the advice he had received, he turned himself into an elk, but instead of passing by, the woman (who was really the sixth giant) came up to him and tearfully reproached him for taking the form of an elk when she had travelled so far to become his wife. Chácopee was so touched by her grief and beauty that he resumed his own shape and endeavoured to console her with gentle words and caresses. At last he fell asleep with his head in her lap. The beautiful woman once more became the cruel giant, and, seizing his axe, the monster broke Chácopee's back; then, turning him into a dog, he bade him rise and follow him. The white feather he stuck in his own head, fancying that magic powers accompanied the wearing of it.

In the path of the travellers there lay a certain village where lived two young sisters, the daughters of a chief. Having heard the prophecy concerning the wearer of the white feather, each made up her mind that she would marry him when he should appear. Therefore, when they saw a man approaching with a white feather in his hair the elder ran to meet him, invited him into her lodge, and soon after married him. The younger, who was gentle and timid, took the dog into her home and treated him with great kindness.

One day while the giant was out hunting he saw the dog casting a stone into the water. Immediately the stone became a beaver, which the dog caught and killed. The giant tried to copy this feat, and was successful, but when he went home and ordered his wife to go outside and fetch the beaver, only a stone lay by the door. Next day he saw the dog plucking a withered branch and throwing it on the ground. It became a deer, which the dog slew. The Giant performed this magic feat also, but when his wife went to the door of the lodge to fetch the deer, she saw only a

The monster turned Chacopee into a dog. Until the advent of the horse, dogs were the only animals domesticated by the Native Americans on any scale.

piece of rotten wood. Nevertheless the giant had some success in the chase, and his wife hurried to the home of her father to tell him what a skilful hunter her husband was. She also spoke of the dog that lived with her sister and his skill in the chase.

The old chief suspected magic, and sent a deputation of youths and maidens to invite his younger daughter and her dog to visit him. To the surprise of the deputation, no dog was there but an exceedingly handsome warrior. But alas! Chácopee could not speak. The party set off for the home of the old chief where they were warmly welcomed.

A general meeting was arranged, where the wearer of the white feather might show his prowess and magical powers. First of all they took the giant's pipe (which had belonged to Chácopee), and the warriors smoked it, one after the other. When it came to Chácopee's turn he signified that the giant should precede him. The giant smoked, but to the disappointment of the assembly nothing unusual happened. Then Chácopee took the pipe, and as the smoke ascended it became a flock of pigeons. At the same moment he recovered his speech, and recounted his strange adventures to the astounded listeners. Their indignation against the giant was unbounded, and the chief ordered that he should be given the form of a dog and stoned to death by the people.

Chácopee gave further proof of his right to wear the white feather. Calling for a buffalo-hide, he cut it into little pieces and strewed it on the prairie. Next day he summoned the braves of the tribe to a buffalo-hunt, and at no great distance they found a magnificent herd. The pieces of hide had become buffaloes. The people greeted this exhibition of magic art with loud praise, and Chácopee's reputation was firmly established with the tribe.

Chácopee begged the chief's permission to take his wife on a visit to his grandfather. This was readily granted, and the old man's gratitude and delight more than repaid them for the perils of their journey.

The Rabbit dwelt in a lodge. A Crow lodge by George Catlin. (Illustration from *Letters on the North American Indians*, 1841.)

Sun image painted on a Mandan buffalo robe by the chief, Mato-tope, about 1832, as a source of power to the wearer.

HOW THE RABBIT CAUGHT THE SUN

Once upon a time the Rabbit dwelt in a lodge with no-one but his grandmother to keep him company. Every morning he went hunting very early, but no matter how early he was, he always noticed that someone with a very long foot had been before him and had left a trail. The Rabbit resolved to discover the identitiy of the hunter who forestalled him, so one fine morning he rose even earlier than usual, in the hope of encountering the stranger. But all to no purpose, for the mysterious one had gone, leaving behind him, as was his wont, the trail of the long foot.

This irritated the Rabbit profoundly, and he returned to the lodge to consult with his grandmother.

"Grandmother," he grumbled, "although I rise early every morning and set my traps in the hope of snaring game, someone is always before me and frightens the game away. I shall make a snare and catch him."

"Why should you do so?" replied his grandmother. "In what way has he harmed you?"

"It is sufficient that I hate him," replied the peevish Rabbit, and departed. He hid himself among the bushes and waited for nightfall. He had provided himself with a stout bowstring, which he arranged as a trap in the place where the footprints were usually to be found. Then he went home, but returned very early to examine his snare.

When he arrived at the spot he discovered that he had caught the intruder, who was, indeed, no less a personage than the Sun. He ran home at the top of his speed to tell his grandmother the news. He did not know what he had caught, so his grandmother bade him return to the forest once more and find out. On returning he saw that the Sun was in a violent passion.

"How dare you snare me!" he cried angrily. "Come here and untie me at once!"

The Rabbit advanced cautiously, and circled round him in abject terror. At last he ducked his head and, running in, cut the bowstring which secured the Sun with his knife. The Sun immediately soared upward, and was quickly lost to sight. And the reason why the hair between the Rabbit's shoulders is yellow is that he was scorched there by the great heat which came from the Sun-god when he freed him.

He summoned the braves of the tribe to a buffalo-hunt. Buffalo-hunting by George Catlin, from *North American Indian Portfolio,* 1844.

CHAPTER 4

MYTHS AND LEGENDS OF THE PAWNEES

A certain young man was very vain of his appearance, and always wore the finest clothes and richest adornments he could procure. Among other possessions he had the down feather of an eagle, which he wore on his head when he went to war and which possessed magical properties. He was unmarried and cared nothing for women, though doubtless there was more than one maiden of the village who would have welcomed the hand of the young hunter, for he was as brave and good-natured as he was handsome.

One day while he was out hunting with his companions—the Indians hunted on foot in those days—he got separated from the others, and followed some buffaloes for a considerable distance. The animals managed to escape, with the exception of a young cow which had become stranded in a mud-hole. The youth fitted an arrow to his bow, and was about to fire when he saw that the buffalo had vanished and only a young and pretty woman was in sight. The hunter was rather perplexed, for he could not understand where the animal had gone to, nor where the woman had come from. However, he talked to the maiden, and found her so agreeable that he proposed to marry her and return with her to his tribe. She consented to marry him, but only on condition that they remained where they were. To this he agreed, and gave her as a wedding gift the string of blue and white beads he wore round his neck.

One evening when he returned home after a day's hunting, he found that his camp was gone, and all round about were the marks of many hoofs. No trace of his wife's body could he discover, and at last, mourning her bitterly, he returned to his tribe.

Years elapsed, and one summer morning as he was playing a stick game with his friends a little boy came towards him, wearing round his neck a string of blue and white beads.

"Father," he said, "mother wants you."

A certain young man " always wore the finest clothes". *Plains Indian with hair-pipe breastplate* by Richard Petri. (Texas Memorial Museum.)

The Grand Canyon of the Yellowstone National Park (opposite) by Thomas Moran (1837–1926), a landscape typical of the edge of the Plains. (Private collection.)

"He was playing a stick game". Lacrosse was an American invention. (Illustration from George Caitlin, *A North American Portfolio*, 1844.)

A string of blue and white beads. Beads made in Italy and Czechoslovakia were traded between Europeans and Native Americans.

The hunter was annoyed at the interruption and spoke roughly to the child. "I am not your father," he said. "Go away and leave me alone."

The boy went away, and the man's companions laughed at him when they heard him addressed as "father," for they knew he was a woman-hater and unmarried.

However, the boy returned in a little while. He was again sent away by the angry hunter, but one of the players now suggested that he should accompany the child and see what he wanted. All the time the hunter had been wondering where he had seen the beads before. As he reflected, he saw a buffalo cow and calf running across the prairie, and suddenly he remembered.

Taking his bow and arrows, he followed the buffaloes, whom he now recognized as his wife and child. A long and wearisome journey they had. The woman was angry with her husband, and dried up every creek they came to, so that he feared he would die of thirst, but his son obtained food and drink for him until they arrived at the home of the buffaloes. The big bulls, the leaders of the herd, were very angry and threatened to kill him. First, however, they gave him a test, telling him that if he accomplished it he should live. Six cows, all exactly alike, were placed in a row, and he was told that if he could point out his wife his life would be spared. His son secretly helped him, and he succeeded. The old bulls were surprised and much annoyed, for they had not expected him to distinguish his wife from the other cows. They gave him another test. He was asked to pick out his son from among several calves. Again the young buffalo helped him to perform the feat. Not yet satisfied, the old bulls decreed that he must run a race. If he should win they would let him go. They chose their fastest runners, but on the day set for the race a thin coating of ice covered the ground, and the buffaloes could not run at all, while the young Indian ran swiftly and steadily and won with ease.

The chief bulls were still angry, however, and determined that they would kill him, even though he had passed their tests. So they made him sit on the ground, all the strongest and fiercest bulls around him. Together they rushed at him, and in a little while his feather was seen floating in the air. The chief bulls called on the others to stop, for they were sure that he must be trampled to pieces by this time. But when they drew back there sat the Indian in the centre of the circle, with his feather in his hair.

It was, in fact, his magic feather to which he owed his escape, and a second rush which the buffaloes made had as little effect on him. Seeing that he was possessed of magical powers, the buffaloes made the best of matters and welcomed him into their camp, on condition that he would bring them gifts from his tribe. This he agreed to do.

When the Indian returned with his wife and son to the village people they found that there was no food to be had, but the buffalo-wife produced some meat from under her robe. Afterwards they went back to the herd with gifts, which greatly pleased the buffaloes. The chief bulls, knowing that the people were in want of food, offered to return with the hunter. His son, who also wished to return, arranged to accompany the herd in the form of a buffalo, while his parents went ahead in human shape. The father warned the people that they must not kill his son when they went to hunt buffaloes, for, he said, the yellow calf would always return leading more buffaloes.

By and by the child came to his father, saying that he would no longer

The woman dried up every creek they came to. In the Pine Ridge area of North Nebraska and South Dakota, erosion has created a barren sandy landscape.

"He saw a buffalo cow and calf running across the prairie." (Illustration from R. I. Dodge, *The Hunting Ground of the Great West*, 1877.)

visit the camp in the form of a boy, as he was about to lead the herd to the east. Before he went he told his father that when the hunters sought the chase they should kill the yellow calf and sacrifice it to Atius Tiráwa, tan its hide, and wrap in the skin an ear of corn and other sacred objects. Every year they should look out for another yellow calf, sacrifice it, and keep a piece of its fat to add to the bundle. Then when food was scarce and famine threatened the tribe the chiefs should gather in council and pay a friendly visit to the young buffalo, and he would tell Tiráwa of their need, so that another yellow calf might be sent to lead the herd to the people.

When he had said this the boy left the camp. All was done as he had ordered. Food became plentiful, and the father became a chief, greatly respected by his people. His buffalo-wife, however, he almost forgot, and one night she vanished. So distressed was the chief, and so remorseful for his neglect of her, that he never recovered, but withered away and died. But the sacred bundle was long preserved in the tribe as a magic charm to bring the buffalo.

THE KINDNESS OF THE BEARS

The chiefs gather in council. (Illustration from the Rev. E. R. Young, *By Canoe and Dog Train among the Cree and Salteaux Indians*, 1903.)

"He accompanied a war party". Armed and provisioned, a war party might expect to be away from home for months. (Illustration from R. I. Dodge, *The Hunting Grounds of the Great West*, 1877.)

There was once a boy of the Pawnee tribe who imitated the ways of a bear; and, indeed, he much resembled that animal. When he played with the other boys of his village he would pretend to be a bear, and even when he grew up he would often laughingly tell his companions that he could turn himself into a bear whenever he liked.

His rememblance to the animal came about in this manner. Before the boy was born his father had gone on the warpath, and at some distance from his home had come upon a tiny bear-cub. The little creature looked at him so wistfully and was so small and helpless that he could not pass by without taking notice of it. So he stooped down and picked it up in his arms, tied some Indian tobacco round its neck, and said: "I know that the

The boy imitated the ways of a bear.
American black bear, from J. J. Audubon,
*The Viviparous Quadrupeds of North
America*, 1846–54.

Great Spirit, Tiráwa, will care for you, but I cannot go on my way without putting these things round your neck to show that I feel kindly toward you. I hope that the animals will take care of my son when he is born, and help him to grow up a great and wise man." With that he went on his way.

On his return he told his wife of his encounter with the Little Bear, told her how he had taken it in his arms and looked at it and talked to it. Now the Indians believed that a woman, before a child is born, must not look fixedly at or think much about any animal, or the infant would resemble it. So when the warrior's son was born, he was found to have the ways of a bear, and to become more and more like that animal the older he grew. The boy, quite aware of the resemblance, often went away by himself into the forest, where he used to pray to the Bear.

On one occasion, when he was quite grown up, he accompanied a war party of the Pawnees as their chief. They travelled a considerable distance, but before they reached any village they fell into a trap prepared for them by their enemies the Sioux. Taken completely off their guard, the Pawnees, around 40 in number, were slain to a man. The part of the country in which this incident took place was rocky and cedar-clad and harboured many bears, and the bodies of the dead Pawnees lay in a ravine in the path of these animals. When they came to the body of the Bear-man, a she-bear instantly recognized it as that of their benefactor, who had sacrificed smokes to them, made songs about them, and done them many a good turn during his lifetime. She called to her companion and begged him to do something to bring the Bear-man to life again. The other protested that there was very little he could do to help her. "Nevertheless," he added, "I will try. If the sun were shining I might succeed, but when it is dark and cloudy I am powerless."

The sun was shining only fitfully that day, however. Long intervals of gloom succeeded each gleam of sunlight. But the two bears set about collecting the remains of the Bear-man, who was sadly mutilated, and, lying down on his body, they worked over him with their magic medicine till he showed signs of returning life. At length he fully regained consciousness, and, finding himself in the presence of two bears, was at a loss to know what had happened to him. But the animals told him how they had brought him to life, and the sight of his dead comrades lying around him reminded him of what had gone before. Gratefully acknowledging the service the bears had done him, he accompanied them to their den. He was still very weak, and frequently fainted, but before long he recovered his strength and was as well as ever, only he had no hair on his head, for the Sioux had scalped him. During his stay with the bears he was taught all the things that they knew—which was a great deal, for all Indians know that the bear is one of the wisest of animals. However, his host begged him not to regard the wonderful things he did as the outcome of his own strength, but to give thanks to Tiráwa, who had made the bears and had given them their wisdom and greatness. Finally he told the Bear-man to return to his own people, where he would become a very great man, both in war and in wealth. But at the same time he must not forget the bears, nor cease to imitate them, for on that would depend much of his success.

"I shall look after you," he concluded. "If I die, you shall die; if I grow old, you shall grow old along with me. This tree"—pointing to a cedar—"shall be a protector to you. It never becomes old; it is always fresh and beautiful, the gift of Tiráwa. And if a thunderstorm should come while you are at home, throw some cedar-wood on the fire and you will be safe."

Giving him a bear-skin cap to hide his hairless scalp, the Bear then bade him depart.

When he arrived at his home, the young man was greeted with amazement, for everyone assumed that he had perished with the rest of the war party. But when he convinced his parents that it was indeed their son

Buffalo meat was dried during the summer when in plentiful supply for use as winter food. (Illustration from R. I. Dodge, *The Hunting Grounds of the Great West*, 1877.)

A grand chief of the Pawnee is
distinguished by the length of his
feathered bonnet. (Illustration from
R. I. Dodge, *The Hunting Grounds of the
Great West*, 1877.)

who visited them, they received him joyfully. When he had embraced
his friends and had been congratulated by them on his return, he told
them about the bears, who were waiting outside the village. Taking pre-
sents of Indian tobacco, sweet-smelling clay, buffalo-meat and beads, he
returned to them, and again talked with the he-bear. The latter hugged
him, saying: "As my fur has touched you, you will be great; as my paws
have touched your hands, you will be fearless; and as my mouth touches
your mouth, you will be wise." With that the bears departed.

True to his words, the animal made the Bear-man the greatest warrior
of his tribe. He was the originator of the Bear Dance, which the Pawnees
still practise. He lived to an advanced age, greatly honoured by his
people.

CHAPTER 5

TALES FROM THE NORTH AND THE PACIFIC COAST

Ten brothers went out to hunt with their dogs. While they were climbing a steep, rocky mountain a thick mist enveloped them, and they were forced to remain on the heights. By and by they made a fire, and the youngest, who was full of mischief, threw his bow in it. When the bow was burnt the hunters were astonished to see it on the level ground below. The mischievous brother thereupon announced his intention of following his weapon, and by the same means. Though the others tried hard to dissuade him, he threw himself on the blazing fire, and was quickly consumed. His brothers then beheld him on the plain, vigorously exhorting them to follow his example. One by one they did so, some boldly, some timorously, but all found themselves at last on the level ground.

As the brothers travelled on they heard a wren chirping, and they saw that one of their number had a blue hole in his heart. Further on they found a hawk's feather, which they tied in the hair of the youngest. They came at length to a deserted village on the shores of an inlet, and took possession of one of the huts. For food they ate some mussels, and having satisfied their hunger, they set out to explore the settlement. Nothing rewarded their search but an old canoe, moss-grown and covered with nettles. When they had removed the weeds and scraped off the moss they repaired it, and the mischievous one who had led them into the fire made a bark bailer for it, on which he carved the representation of a bird. Another, who had in his hair a bunch of feathers, took a pole and jumped into the canoe. The rest followed, and the canoe slid away from the shore.

Soon they came in sight of a village where a medicine man was performing. Attracted by the noise and the glow of the fire, the warrior at the bow stepped ashore and advanced to see what was going on. "Now," he heard the medicine man say, "the chief Supernatural-being-who-keeps-the-bow-off is coming ashore." The Indian was ashamed to hear himself thus mistakenly (as he thought) referred to as a supernatural being, and

A Tlingit chief's blanket woven from cedar bark fibre and mountain goat's hair. (Smithsonian, *Report of the National Museum*, 1894.)

Nespilim girl (opposite) from a tribe living north of the Columbia River in the Nespilim valley. (Illustration from Edward Curtis, *The North American Indian*, 1907–30.)

View of the Rocky Mountains by Albert Bierstadt (1830–1902). The Rocky Mountains marked the eastern boundary of the lands occupied by the Northwest tribes. (White House, Washington, D.C., North America.)

returned to the canoe. The next one advanced to the village. "Chief Hawk-hole is coming ashore," said the medicine man. The Indian saw the blue hole at his heart, and he also was ashamed and returned to his brothers. The third was named Supernatural-being-on-whom-the-daylight-rests, the fourth Supernatural-being-on-the-water-on-whom-is-sunshine, the fifth Supernatural-puffin-on-the-water, the sixth Hawk-with-one-feather-sticking-out-of-the-water, the seventh Wearing-clouds-around-his-neck, the eighth Supernatural-being-with-the-big-eyes, the ninth Supernatural-being-lying-on-his-back-in-the-canoe, and the eldest, and last, Supernatural-being-half-of-whose-words-are-raven. Each as he heard his name pronounced, returned to the canoe as his brother had done before him. When they had all heard the medicine man, and were assembled once more, the eldest brother said, "We have indeed become supernatural people," which was quite true, for by burning themselves in the blazing fire they had reached the Land of Souls.

The ten brothers floated round the coast till they reached another village. Here they took on board a woman whose arms had been accidentally burned by her husband, having mistaken them for the arms of some one embracing his wife. The woman was severely burned and was in great distress. The supernatural brothers made a crack in the bottom of the canoe and told the woman to place her hands in it. Her wounds were immediately healed. They called her their sister, and seated her in the canoe to bail out the water. When they came to the Djū, the stream near which dwelt Fine-weather-woman, the latter came and talked to them, repeating the names which the medicine man had given them, and calling their sister Supernatural-woman-who-does-the-bailing.

"Paddle to the island you see in the distance," she added. "The wizard who lives there paints those who are to become supernatural beings. Go to him and he will paint you. Dance four nights in your canoe and you will be finished."

They did as she bade them, and the wizard dressed them in a manner becoming to their position as supernatural beings. He gave them dancing hats, dancing skirts and puffin-beak rattles, and drew a cloud over the outside of their canoe.

THE SKY-GOD

The daughter of a certain chief went one day to dig on the beach. After she had worked some time she dug up a cockle-shell. She was about to throw it to one side when she thought she heard a sound coming from it like that of a child crying. Examining the shell, she found a tiny baby inside. She carried it home and wrapped it in a warm covering, and tended it so carefully that it grew rapidly and soon began to walk.

She was sitting beside the child one day when he made a movement with his hand as if imitating the drawing of a bowstring, so to please him she took a copper bracelet from her arm and hammered it into the shape of a bow, which she strung and gave him, along with two arrows. He was delighted with the tiny weapon, and immediately set out to hunt small game with it. Every day he returned to his foster-mother with some trophy of his skill. One day it was a goose, another a woodpecker, another a blue jay.

One morning he awoke to find himself and his mother in a fine new house, with gorgeous door-posts splendidly carved and painted in rich reds, blues and greens. The carpenter who had raised this fine building married the boy's foster-mother, and was very kind to him. He took the boy down to the sea-shore and caused him to sit with his face looking toward the expanse of the Pacific. And as long as the lad remained in this position,

The woman took a copper bracelet. Copper working began in North America among the people of the Great Lakes as early as 5000–3000 B.C. The metal was not smelted but hammered flat.

The shores of an inlet (left). In an area of dense forest and rocky terrain, most people travelled along the coast and rivers and built their villages near water.

facing the boundless blue ocean, there was fair weather.

His father used to go fishing, and one day Sîñ—for such was the boy's name—expressed a wish to accompany him. They took devil-fish for bait, and proceeded to the fishing-ground, where the lad instructed his father to repeat certain magical formulæ. The result of this was that their fishing-line was violently agitated and their canoe pulled round an adjacent island three times. When the disturbance stopped at last, they pulled in the line and dragged out a monster covered with piles of halibut.

One day Sîñ went out wearing a wren-skin. His mother beheld him rise in stature until he soared above her and floated like a bank of shining clouds over the ocean. Then he descended and donned the skin of a blue jay. Again he rose over the sea, and shone brilliantly. Once more he soared upward, wearing the skin of a woodpecker, and the waves reflected the colours of fire.

Then he said: "Mother, I shall see you no more. I am going away from you. When the sky looks like my face painted by my father there will be no wind. Then the fishing will be good."

His mother bade him farewell, sadly, yet with the proud knowledge that she had nurtured a divinity. But her sorrow increased when her husband told her that it was time for him to depart as well. Her supernatural son and husband, however, did leave her a portion of their power. For when she sits by the inlet and loosens her robe, the wind scurries down between the banks and the waves are ruffled with tempest, and the more she loosens the garment the greater is the storm. They call her in the Indian tongue Fine-weather-woman. But she dwells mostly in the winds,

Door posts "splendidly carved and painted" frequently depicted mythical characters, while painting on the planking of house fronts showed their owner's lineage. (Smithsonian, *Report of the National Museum*, 1894.)

Burger

and when the cold morning airs draw up from the sea towards the land she makes an offering of feathers to her glorious son. The feathers are flakes of snow, and they serve to remind him that the world is weary for a glimpse of his golden face.

Haida portrait mask (left) painted with symbols depicting the crest of the character being portrayed. Such masks often had the same designs as were used in facial painting. (McCord Museum, Montreal.)

MASTER-CARPENTER AND SOUTH-EAST

Master-carpenter, a supernatural being, went to war with the south-east wind at Sqa-i, the town lying farthest south on the Queen Charlotte Islands. The south-east wind is particularly rude and boisterous on that coast, and it was with the intention of punishing him for his violence that Master-carpenter challenged him. First of all, however, he set about building a canoe for himself. The first one he made split and he was obliged to throw it away. The second also split, even though he had made it stouter than the other. Another and another he built, making each one stronger than the last, but every attempt ended in failure, and at last, exceedingly vexed at his incompetence, he was on the point of giving up the task. He would have done so, indeed, but for the intervention of Greatest Fool. Hitherto Master-carpenter had been trying to form two canoes from one log by means of wedges. Greatest Fool stood watching him for a time, amused

Sunset in the Queen Charlotte Islands, home of the Haida people. The unpredictability of the waters in this area of the Pacific demanded special skill in the use of canoes.

121

A good canoe. To make a canoe, usually from cedar wood, required the use of wooden wedges, an adze and steam to expand the wood into its final shape. (Illustration from Edward Curtis, *The North American Indian*, 1907–30.)

Mount St Helens, Washington State. Active volcanoes in the Northwest of America encouraged the creation of such legendary figures as Tidal-Wave and Volcano-Woman.

at his clumsiness, and finally showed him that he ought to use bent wedges. And though he was perhaps the last person from whom Master-carpenter might expect to learn anything, the unsuccessful canoe builder adopted the suggestion, with the happiest of results. When at length he was satisfied that he had made a good canoe, he let it down into the water and sailed off in search of South-east.

By and by he floated right down to his enemy's abode, and when he judged himself to be above it, he rose in the canoe and shouted out a challenge. There was no reply. Again he called, and this time a rapid current began to float past him, bearing on its surface a quantity of seaweed. The shrewd Master-carpenter fancied he saw the matted hair of his enemy floating among the seaweed. He seized hold of it, and after it came South-east. The latter, in a great passion, began to call on his nephews to help him. The first to be summoned was Red-storm-cloud. Immediately a deep red flooded the sky. Then the stormy tints died away, and the wind rose with a harsh murmur. When this wind had reached its full strength another was summoned, Taker-off-of-the-tree-tops. The blast increased to a hurricane, and the tree-tops were blown off and carried away and fell thickly about the canoe, where Master-carpenter was making use of his magic arts to protect himself. Yet another wind was called up, Pebble-rattler, who set the stones and sand flying about as he shrieked in answer to the summons. Maker-of-the-thick-sea-mist came next, the spirit of the fog which strikes terror into the hearts of those at sea, and he was followed by a numerous band of other nephews, each more terrifying than the last. Finally Tidal-wave came and covered Master-carpenter with water, so that he was obliged to give in. Relinquishing his hold on South-east, he managed to struggle to the shore. It was said by some that South-east died, but the medicine men, who ought to know, say that he returned to his own place.

South-east's mother was named Tomorrow, and the Indians say that if they utter that word they will have bad weather, for South-east does not like to hear his mother's name used by anyone else.

BLUE JAY AND IOI

Blue Jay, whose disposition resembled that of the totem-bird he symbolized, delighted in tormenting his sister Ioi by deliberately misinterpreting her commands, and by repeating at every opportunity his favourite phrase, "Ioi is always telling lies."

One day Ioi requested her brother to take a wife from among the dead, to help her with her work in house and field. To this Blue Jay readily assented, and he took for his spouse a chieftain's daughter who had been recently buried. But he ignored Ioi's request that his wife should be an old one.

"Take her to the Land of the Supernatural People," said Ioi, when she

Blue Jay is a trickster, able to change in and out of human form, whose adventures often result in transformations to the natural world. (Illustration from Mark Catesby, *The Natural History of Carolina, Florida and the Bahama Islands*, 1731–43.)

had seen her brother's bride, "and they will restore again her to life."

Blue Jay set out on his errand, and after a day's journey arrived with his wife at a town inhabited by the Supernatural Folk.

"How long has she been dead?" they asked him, when he stated his purpose in visiting them.

"A day," he replied.

The Supernatural People shook their heads.

"We cannot help you," said they. "You must travel to the town where people are restored who have been dead for a day."

Blue Jay obediently resumed his journey, and at the end of another day he reached the town to which he had been directed, and told its inhabitants why he had come.

"How long has she been dead?" they asked.

"Two days," said he.

"Then we can do nothing," replied the Supernatural Folk, "for we can only restore people who have been dead one day. However, you can go to the town where those are brought to life who have been dead two days."

Another day's journey brought Blue Jay and his wife to the third town. Again he found himself a day late, and was directed to a fourth town, and from that one to yet another. At the fifth town, however, the Supernatural People took pity on him, and recovered his wife from death. They made Blue Jay a chieftain among them, and conferred many honours upon him.

Fallen mortuary pole, Skedans village, Queen Charlotte Islands. When high-ranking people died, poles were erected to show respect to their spirits.

After a time Blue Jay got tired of living in state among the Supernatural People, and he returned home with his wife.

When he was once more among his kindred his young brother-in-law, the chief's son, learned that his sister was alive and married to Blue Jay.

Hastily the boy carried the news to his father, the old chief, who sent a message to Blue Jay demanding his hair in payment for his wife. The messenger received no reply, and the angry chief gathered his people round him and led them to Blue Jay's lodge. On their approach Blue Jay turned himself into a bird and flew away, while his wife swooned. All the efforts of her kindred could not bring the woman round, and they called on her husband to return. It was in vain, however: Blue Jay would not come back, and his wife journeyed finally to the Land of Souls.

The Chinooks were a trading people who acted as middlemen between the coastal areas and the tribes living further inland. This view of the Mount Rainier National Park shows a landscape some hundred miles from the sea.

Ioi in the Ghost-Country

The Ghost-people, setting out one night to buy a wife, took Blue Jay's sister Ioi. After a year had elapsed her brother decided to go in search of her. But though he inquired the way to the Ghost-country from all manner of birds and beasts, he got a satisfactory answer from none of them, and would never have arrived at his destination at all had he not been carried there by supernatural means.

In the Ghost-country he found his sister surrounded by heaps of bones, which she introduced to him as his relatives by marriage. At certain times these relics would attain a semblance of humanity. However, they

Whale-catching required the use of unwieldy harpoons equipped with seal-skin floats. (Illustration of whaling crew from Cape Prince of Wales, from Edward Curtis, *The North American Indian*, 1907–30.)

would instantly become bones again at the sound of a loud voice.

At his sister's request Blue Jay went fishing with his young brother-in-law. Finding that when he spoke in a loud tone he caused the boy to become a heap of bones in the canoe, Blue Jay took a malicious pleasure in reducing him to that condition. It was just the sort of trick he loved to play.

The "fish" they caught were nothing more than leaves and branches, and Blue Jay, in disgust, threw them back into the water. But, to his chagrin, when he returned his sister told him that they were really fish, and that he ought not to have flung them away. However, he consoled himself with the reflection "Ioi is always telling lies."

Besides teasing Ioi, he played many pranks on the inoffensive Ghosts. Sometimes he would put the skull of a child on the shoulders of a man, and *vice versa*, and take a mischievous delight in the ludicrous result when they came "alive."

On one occasion, when the prairies were on fire Ioi bade her brother extinguish the flames. For this purpose she gave him five buckets of water, warning him that he must not pour it on the burning prairies until he came to the fourth of them. Blue Jay disobeyed her, as he was wont to do, and with dire results, for when he reached the fifth prairie he found he had no water to pour on it. While endeavouring to beat out the flames he was so seriously burned that he died, and returned to the Ghosts as one of themselves, but without losing his mischievous traits.

Blue Jay's Tests

A messenger from the Divine People approached Blue Jay's people and asked whether the Indians would accept a challenge to a diving contest, the defeated to lose their lives. This was agreed to, and Blue Jay was selected to dive for the Chinooks. He had taken the precaution of placing some bushes in his canoe, which he threw into the water before diving with his opponent, a woman. When his breath gave out he came to the surface, concealing his head under the floating bushes. Then he sank into the water again, and cried to his opponent: "Where are you?" "Here I am," she replied. Four times did Blue Jay cunningly come up for breath, hidden beneath the bushes, and on diving for the last time he found the woman lying at the bottom of the sea, almost unconscious. He took the club, which he had concealed beneath his blanket, and struck her on the nape of the neck. Then he rose and claimed the victory.

The Supernatural People, much chagrined, next suggested a climbing contest. Blue Jay readily agreed, but he was warned that if he was beaten he would be dashed to pieces. He placed upright a piece of ice which was so high that it reached the clouds. The Supernaturals matched a chipmunk against him. When the competitors had reached a certain height Blue Jay grew tired, so he used his wings and flew upward. The chipmunk had her eyes closed, and did not notice the deception. Blue Jay hit her on the neck with his club so that she fell, and Blue Jay was pronounced the winner.

Detail of totem pole in Gitanmaks, British Columbia. The figures represent creatures called "small children".

Killer-whale crest post. This carving was used as part of a memorial at the grave of a Tlingit chief, probably to show his clan affiliation.

A shooting match was next proposed by the exasperated Supernaturals. This the Chinooks won by taking a beaver as their champion and tying a millstone in front of him. A sweating match was also won by the Chinooks, who took ice with them into the superheated caves where the contest took place.

As a last effort to shame the Chinooks, the Divine People suggested that the two chiefs should engage in a whalecatching contest. This was agreed, and the Supernatural chief's wife, after warning them, placed Blue Jay and Robin under her arms to keep them quiet. As they descended to the beach, she said to her brother: "Four whales will pass you, but do not harpoon any until the fifth appears."

Robin did as he was bid, but the woman had a hard time keeping the curious Blue Jay hidden. The four whales passed, but the young chief took no heed. Then the fifth slid by. He thrust his harpoon deep into its blubber and cast it ashore. The Supernatural chief was unsuccessful in his attempts, and so the Chinooks won again. On the result being known Blue Jay could no longer be restrained, and, falling out from under the woman's arm, he was drowned.

On setting out for home, the chief was advised to tie Robin's blanket to a magical rope which his sister gave him. When the Chinooks were in the middle of the ocean, the Supernatural People raised a great storm to bring about their destruction. But the charm the chief's sister had given them proved very effective and they reached their own land in safety.

THE GLUTTON

There were five brothers who lived together. Four of them were accustomed to spend their days in hunting elk, while the fifth, who was the youngest, was always compelled to remain at the camp. They lived amicably enough, save that the youngest grumbled at never being able to go hunting. One day as the youth sat brooding over his grievance, the silence was suddenly broken by a hideous din, which appeared to come from the region of the doorway. He was at a loss to understand the cause of it, and anxiously wished for the return of his brothers. Suddenly there appeared before him a man of gigantic size, strangely clothed. He demanded food, and the frightened boy, remembering that they were well provided, hastily arose to satisfy the stranger's desires. He brought out an ample supply of meat and tallow, but was astonished to find that the strange being lustily called for more. The youth, thoroughly terrified, hastened to gratify the monster's craving, and the giant ate steadily on, hour after hour, until the brothers returned at the end of the day to discover the glutton devouring the fruits of their hunting. The monster appeared not to heed the brothers, but, anxious to satisfy his enormous appetite, he ate on. A fresh supply of meat had been secured and this the brothers placed before him.

He continued to gorge himself throughout the night and well into the next day. At last the meat was at an end, and the brothers became alarmed. What would the insatiable creature demand next? They

Moose-hunting demanded special techniques, including the use of a birch-bark calling horn to attract the animals. (Illustration from the Marquis of Lorne, *Canadian Pictures*, c. 1884.)

approached him and told him that only skins remained, but he replied "What shall I eat, grandchildren, now that there are only skins and you?" They did not appear to understand him until they had questioned him several times. On realizing that the glutton meant to devour them, they determined to escape. Boiling the skins, which they set before him, they fled through a hole in the hut. Outside they placed a dog, and told him to send the giant in the direction opposite to that which they had taken. Night fell, and the monster slept, while the dog kept a weary vigil over the exit by which his masters had escaped. Day dawned as the giant crept through the gap. He asked the dog: "Which way went your masters?" The animal replied by setting his head in the direction opposite to the true one. The giant observed the sign, and went on the road the dog indicated. After proceeding for some distance he realized that the young men could not have gone that way, so he returned to the hut, to find the dog still there. Again he questioned the animal, who merely repeated his previous movement. The monster once more set out, but, unable to discover the fugitives, he again returned. Three times he repeated his fruitless journeys. At last he succeeded in getting on the right path, and very shortly came within sight of the brothers.

Immediately they saw their pursuer, they tried to outrun him, but without avail. The giant gained ground and soon overtook the eldest, whom he killed. He then made for the others, and killed three more, until only the youngest was left. The boy hurried on until he came to a river, on the bank of which was a man fishing. This man's name was the Thunderer. The boy implored the man to convey him to the opposite side. After much hesitation the Thunderer agreed, and rowing him across the

Esquimaux dog by J. J. Audubon from *The Viviparous Quadrupeds of North America*, 1846–54.

Daggers with sheaths of buckskin and moose hide and carved handles. (Smithsonian, *Report of the National Museum*, 1894.)

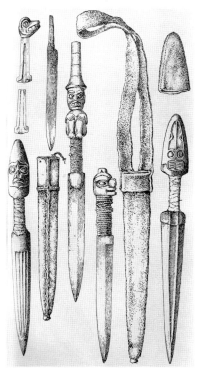

The Thunderer. It was widely believed that thunderstorms were caused by a giant bird. This spindle whorl with a Thunderbird carving was made by the Salish people. (Provincial Museum, British Columbia.)

stream, he commanded the fugitive to go to his hut, and returned to his nets. By this time the monster had reached the river, and on seeing the fisherman he asked to be ferried over also. The Thunderer at first refused, but was eventually persuaded by the offer of a piece of twine. Afraid that the boat might capsize the Thunderer stretched himself across the river, and commanded the giant to walk over his body. The monster, unaware of treachery, readily responded, but no sooner had he reached the Thunderer's legs than the latter set them apart, thus catapulting him into the water. His hat fell in after him. The Thunderer gained his feet, and watched the giant drifting helplessly down the stream. He did not wish to save the monster, for he believed him to be an evil spirit. "Okulam [the noise of a surge] will be your name," he said. "Only when the storm is raging will you be heard. When the weather is very bad your hat will also be heard." As he concluded this prophecy the giant disappeared from sight. The Thunderer then gathered his nets together and went to his hut.

The youth whom he had saved married his daughter, and remained with him. One day the youth wished to watch his father-in-law fishing for whales. His wife warned him against doing so. He paid no heed to her warning, however, but went to the sea, where he saw the Thunderer struggling with a whale. His father-in-law flew into a great rage, and a furious storm arose. The Thunderer looked towards the land, and immediately the storm increased in fury, with thunder and lightning, so he threw down his dip-net and departed for home, followed by his son-in-law.

On reaching the house, the young man gathered some pieces of coal and climbed a mountain. There he blackened his face, and a high wind arose which carried everything before it. His father-in-law's house was blown away, and the Thunderer, seeing that it was hopeless to attempt to save anything from the wreck, commanded his daughter to look for her husband. She hurried up the mountainside, where she found him. She told him that he was the cause of all the destruction, but concluded: "Father says you may look at him tomorrow when he catches whales." He followed his wife back to the valley and washed his face. Immediately he had done so, the storm abated. Going up to his father-in-law, he said: "Tomorrow I shall go down to the beach, and you shall see me catching whales." Then he and the Thunderer rebuilt their hut. On the following morning they went down to the sea-shore together. The young man cast his net into the sea. After a little while a whale entered the net. The youth quickly pulled the net towards him, reached for the whale, and flung it at the feet of his father-in-law. Thunderer was amazed, and called to him "Ho, my son-in-law, you are just as I was when I was a young man."

Thunderer's Son-in-law

The Thunderer then sent his son-in-law to split a log of wood. When this had been done, he put the young man's strength to the test by placing him within the hollow trunk and closing the wood around him. But the young man succeeded in freeing himself, and set off for the hut, carrying the log with him. On reaching home he dropped the wood before the door, and

"Okulam [the noise of a surge] will be your name." In many Northwest myths natural features were active characters. This river and woodland scene is typical of Washington State.

Tlingit stone pipe showing a whale chasing a seal. The whale's head contains the pipe bowl, while the mouthpiece is between the seal's head and the whale's tail. (British Museum.)

Totem poles (opposite) near a Haida village. Carved with the crests of supernatural animals or totem spirits, such posts served as memorials of peoples and of special events.

caused the earth to quake. The Thunderer jumped up in alarm and ran to the door, rejoicing in the might of his son-in-law. "Oh, my son-in-law," he cried, "you are just as I was when I was young!" The two continued to live together and the young man's sons grew into manhood.

One day the Thunderer approached his son-in-law and said, "Go to the Supernatural Folk and bring me their hoops." The son-in-law obeyed. He travelled for a long distance, and eventually reached the land of the spirits. They stood in a circle, and he saw that they played with a large hoop. He then remembered that he must secure the hoop, but he was afraid to approach them, as the light of the place dazzled him. He waited until darkness had set in and, leaving his hiding-place, dashed through the circle and secured the hoop. The Supernatural People pursued him with torches.

Just as this was taking place his wife remembered him, and she called to her children: "Now whip your grandfather." This they did, while the old man wept. This chastisement brought rain upon the Supernatural People and extinguished their torches. They dared not pursue the young man farther, so they returned to their country. The adventurer was now left in peace to continue his homeward journey. He handed over the hoop to Thunderer, who now sent him to capture the targets of the Spirit Folk. The son-in-law gladly undertook the journey, and again entered the bright region of Spirit-land. He found the Supernaturals shooting at the targets, and when night had fallen he picked them up and ran away. The spirits lit their torches and followed him. His wife once more was reminded of her absent husband, and commanded her sons to repeat the punishment upon their grandfather. The rain recommenced and the torches of the pursuers were destroyed. The young man returned in peace to his dwelling and placed the targets before his father-in-law.

He had not been long home before a restless spirit took possession of him. He longed for further adventure, and at last decided to set out in quest of it. Arraying himself in his fine necklaces of teeth and strapping around his waist two quivers of arrows, he bade farewell to his wife and sons. He journeyed until he reached a large village, which consisted of five rows of houses. These he carefully inspected. The last house was very small, but he entered it. He was met by two old women, who were known as the Mice. Immediately they saw him, they muttered to each other: "Now Blue Jay will make another chief unhappy." On the young man's arrival in the village, Blue Jay became conscious of a stranger in the midst of the people. He straight away hurried to the house of the Mice. He then returned to his chief saying that a strange chief wished to hold a shooting match. Blue Jay's chief seemed quite willing to enter into the contest with the stranger, so he sent Blue Jay back to the house to inform the young chief of his willingness. Blue Jay led the stranger down to the beach where the targets stood. Soon the old chief arrived and the shooting match began, but the adventurer's skill could not compare with the old chief's, who finally defeated him.

Blue Jay now saw his opportunity. He sprang upon the stranger, tore out his hair, cut off his head, and severed the limbs from his body. He carried the pieces to the house and hung up the head, but at night-fall the Mice fed the head and managed to keep it alive. This process of feeding went on for many months, the old women never tiring of their task. A full year had passed, and the unfortunate adventurer's sons began to fear for his safety. They decided to search for him. Arming themselves, they made their way to the large village in which their father was imprisoned. They entered the house of the Mice, and there saw the two old women, who asked: "Oh, chiefs, where did you come from?"

"We search for our father," they replied. But the old women warned them of Blue Jay's treachery, and advised them to depart. The young men would not heed the advice, and succeeded in drawing from the women the story of their father's fate. When they heard that Blue Jay had used their father so badly they were very angry. Blue Jay, meanwhile, had

A Haida shaman's rattle (far right), carved with a different design on each side. A small face can be seen inside the mouth of the larger head. (National Museum of Man, Ottowa.)

Reverse side of rattle (right). Rattles of this kind were usually carved from two pieces of wood which were then tied together round the pebbles which made the noise.

In the subarctic north (left), nomadic peoples following the herds of caribou lived in tepees. (Illustration from the Marquis of Lorne, *Canadian Pictures, c.* 1884.)

An Indian of the North-West Territories of Canada. (Illustration from the Marquis of Lorne, *Canadian Pictures, c.* 1884.)

become aware of the arrival of two strangers, and he went to the small house to smell them out. There he espied the youths, and immediately returned to inform his chief of their presence in the village. The chief sent him back to invite the strangers to a shooting match, but they ignored the invitation.

Three times Blue Jay made the journey, and at last the youths looked upon him, whereupon his hair immediately caught fire. He ran back to his chief and said: "These strangers are more powerful than we are. They looked at me and my hair caught fire." The chief was amazed, and went

"The chief went down to the beach."
Kamloops Lake, British Columbia.
"Kamloops" means "the meeting of the
waters".

down to the beach to await the arrival of the strangers. When the young men saw the targets they would not shoot, and declared that they were bad. They immediately drew them out of the ground and replaced them by their own, the brilliance of which dazzled the sight of their opponent. The chief was defeated. He lost his life and the people were subdued. The youths then cast Blue Jay into the river, saying as they did so: "Green Sturgeon shall be your name. Henceforth you shall not make chiefs miserable. You shall sing 'Watsetsetsetsetse', and it shall be a bad omen." This performance over, they restored their father from his death-slumber, and spoke kindly to the Mice, saying: "Oh, you pitiful ones, you shall eat everything that is good. You shall eat berries." Then after establishing order in this strange land, they returned to their home, accompanied by their father.

OUIOT, THE GRAND CAPTAIN

Before the material world existed, there lived two beings, brother and sister, of a nature that cannot be explained; the brother living above, his name meaning the Heavens, the sister living below, her name signifying Earth. From the union of these two there sprang numerous offspring. Earth and sand were the first fruits of this marriage; then were born rocks and stones; then trees, both great and small; then grass and herbs; then animals: Lastly was born a great personage called Ouiot, who was a "grand captain." By some unknown mother, many children of a medicine race were born to this Ouiot. All these things happened in the north; and afterwards, when men were created, they were created in the north; but as the people multiplied they moved toward the south, the earth growing larger also and extending itself in the same direction.

In the process of time, Ouiot became old and his children plotted to kill him, alleging that the infirmities of age made him unfit to govern them or attend to their welfare. So they put a strong poison in his drink, and when he drank of it a sore sickness came upon him; he rose up and left his home in the mountains, and went down to what is now the seashore, though at that time there was no sea there. His mother, whose name is the Earth, mixed him an antidote in a large shell, and set the potion out in the sun to brew, but the fragrance of it attracted the attention of the Coyote, who came and overset the shell. So Ouiot sickened to death, and though he told his children that he would shortly return and be with them again, he has never been seen since. All the villagers made a great pile of wood and burned his body there, and just as the ceremony began the Coyote leaped upon the body, saying that he would burn with it, but he only tore a piece of flesh from the stomach and ate it and escaped. After that the title of the Coyote was changed from Eyacque, which means Sub-captain, to Eno, that is to say, Thief and Cannibal.

When the funeral rites were over, a general council was held and arrangements made for collecting animal and vegetable food; up to this time the children and descendants of Ouiot had nothing to eat but a kind of white clay. And while they consulted together, a marvellous thing appeared before them, and they spoke to it, saying: "Are you our captain, Ouiot?" But the spectre said "No, for I am greater than Ouiot; my habitation is above and my name is Chinigchinich." Then he spoke further, having been told why they were come together: "I create all things and I go now to make man, another people like you; as for you, I give you power, each after his kind, to produce all good and pleasant things. One of you shall bring rain, and another dew, and another make the acorn grow, and others other seeds, and yet others shall cause all kinds of game to abound in the land, and your children shall have this power forever, and they shall be sorcerers to the men I go to create, and shall receive gifts of them, that the game fail not and the harvests be sure." Then Chinigchinich made humans; out of the clay of the lake he formed them, male and female, and the present Californians are the descendants of the one or more pairs there and thus created.

"Men were created in the north." The first Americans probably settled in Alaska after crossing the Bering Strait from northeast Asia. Mentesta Lake, Alaska.

Ouiot left his home in the mountains and went to what is now the seashore. Rocky coast near Fort Ross, California.

NOCUMA

The people of the valley of San Juan Capistrano say that an invisible, all-powerful being, called Nocuma, made the world and all that it contains of things that grow and move. He made it round like a ball and held it in his hands, where it rolled about a good deal at first, till he steadied it by sticking a heavy black rock called Tosaut into it, as a kind of ballast. The sea was at this time only a little stream running round the world, and so

The Pomo peoples of California were renowned for their basketry and made shelters, clothing and even canoes out of reeds, grasses and wood. (Illustration from Edward Curtis, *The North American Indian*, 1907–30.)

crowded with fish that their twinkling fins had no longer room to move; so great was the crush that some of the more foolish fish were for effecting a landing and founding a colony upon the dry land, and it was only with the utmost difficulty that they were persuaded by their elders that the air and sun must infallibly prove their destruction before many days. The proper plan was evidently to improve and enlarge their present home; and to this end, principally with the aid of one very large fish, they broke the great rock Tosaut in two, finding a bladder in the centre filled with a very bitter substance. The taste of it pleased the fish, so they emptied it into the water, and instantly the water became salt and swelled up and overflowed a great part of the old earth, and made itself the new boundaries that remain to this day.

Then Nocuma created a man, shaping him out of the soil of the earth and calling him Ejoni. A woman also was made, out of the same material as the man, caled Aé. Many children were born to this first pair, and their descendants multiplied over the land. The name of one of these last was Sirout, that is to say, Handful of Tobacco, and the name of his wife was Ycaiut, which means Above; and to Sirout and Ycaiut was born a son, while they lived in a place north-east about eight leagues from San Juan Capistrano. The name of this son was Ouiot, that is to say, Dominator; he grew to be a fierce and redoubtable warrior; haughty, ambitious, tyrannous, he extended his lordship on every side, ruling everywhere as with a rod of iron and the people conspired against him. It was decided that he should die by poison; a piece of the rock Tosaut was ground up in so deadly a way that its mere external application was sufficient to cause death. Ouiot (even though he held himself constantly on the alert, having been warned of his danger by a small animal called the *cucumel*) was unable to avoid his fate; a few grains of the mixture were dropped upon his breast while he slept, and the strong mineral ate its way to the very springs of his life. All the wise men of the land were called to his assistance; but there was nothing anyone could do. His body was burned on a great pile with songs of joy and dances, and the nation rejoiced.

While the people were thus gathered together it was thought advisable to consult on the feasibility of procuring seed and flesh to eat instead of the clay which had up to this time been the sole food of the human family. And while they talked together, there suddenly appeared to them one called Attajen, which name implies man, or rational being. And Attajen, understanding their desires, chose certain elders from among them, and to these men he gave power; one that he might cause rain to fall, to another that he might cause game to abound, and so with the rest, to each his power and gift and to the successors of each for ever. These were the first medicine-men.

THE STORY OF QUAAYAYP

There was a great lord in heaven called Niparaya, who made earth and sea, and was almighty and invisible. His wife was Anayicoyondi, a goddess who, though possessing no body, bore him in a divinely mysterious manner three children, one of whom, Quaayayp, was a real man and born on earth, on the Acaragui mountains. Very powerful this young god was, and for a long time he lived with the ancestors of the Pericues. The men at last killed their great hero and teacher, and put a crown of thorns upon his head. Somewhere or other he remains lying dead to this day, and he remains constantly beautiful, neither does his body know corruption. Blood drips constantly from his wounds; and though he can speak no more, being dead, yet there is an owl that speaks to him.

Owl ornament from the prow of Tlingit war canoe, inlaid with abalone shell and trimmed with bear fur. (Field Museum of Natural History, Chicago.)

GREAT SHOE

The Loucheux tribe recognized a certain personage, resident in the moon, to whom they prayed for success when starting on a hunting expedition. This being once lived among them as a poor ragged boy that an old woman had found and was bringing up, and who made himself ridiculous to his fellows by making a pair of very large snow-shoes; for the people could not see what a orphan like he should want with shoes of such unusual size. Times of great scarcity troubled the hunters, and they would often have fared badly had they not, invariably on such occasions, come across a new broad trail that led to a head or two of freshly killed game. They were glad

An owl speaks to the dead Quaayayp.
Owls were widely believed to associate
with the spirits of the dead. Little owl
by Mark Catesby from *The Natural
History of Carolina, Florida and the
Bahama Islands*, 1731–43.

Very large snow shoes. Generally made
from hide lacing on a wooden frame,
the size and shape of snow shoes
varied according to terrain and snow
density. (Illustration from George
Caitlin, *Letters on the North American
Indians*, 1841.)

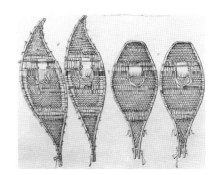

enough to get the game and without scruples as to its appropriation; still
they felt curious as to whence it came and how.

Suspicion at last pointed to the boy and his great shoes as being in some
way implicated in the affair, and he was watched. It soon became evident
that he was indeed the benefactor of the Loucheux, and the secret hunter
whose quarry had so often replenished their empty pots, yet the people
were far from being adequately grateful, and continued to treat him with
little kindness or respect. On one occasion they refused him a certain piece
of fat—he who had so often saved their lives by his timely bounty! That
night the boy disappeared, leaving only his clothes behind, hanging on a
tree. He returned to them in a month, however, appearing as a man, and
dressed as a man. He told them that he had taken up his home in the
moon, that he would always look down with a kindly eye to their success
in hunting, but he added that as a punishment for their shameless greed
and ingratitude in refusing him the piece of fat, all animals should be
lean the long winter through, and fat only in summer, as has been the case
ever since.

Nunivak child (opposite). Nunivak
Island lies in the Bering Sea off the
western coast of Alaska. (Illustration
from Edward Curtis, *The North
American Indian*, 1907–30.)

INDEX

INDEX

An oasis in the Bad Lands. (Photograph by Edward Curtis, 1905, from *The North American Indian*.)

ACKNOWLEDGEMENTS

The Bridgeman Art Library, London: 19, 23, 38, 41, 77, 85, 89, 101, 108, 118; Canada House, London: 63, 119, 133; J Allan Cash: 11 (top), 17 (left), 41, 43, 47, 48, 52, 55, 61 (left), 93, 111, 121, 137; Werner Forman, London: 4, 59 (bottom), 121 (left), 124, 127, 130, 132, 134, 139; Fotomas Index, London: 8, 22 (bottom), 45 (top), 69, 91 (bottom), 105, 124, 139; Robert Francis, London: 10 (bottom), 13 (top), 43 (left), 90, 102, 122 (bottom), 125, 131, 136; Joslyn Art Museum, Omaha: 87 (bottom); Mansell Collection, London: 10, 11 (right), 12, 88; MPL, Bath: 9 (right), 19 (top), 41, 43, 52 (left), 59, 69, 79, 83, 84 (bottom), 89, 91 (top), 96, 99 (top), 106, 111, 112, 114, 115, 117, 120, 129, 141; National Film Board of Canada: 63, 119, 133; Pitt-Rivers Museum, Oxford: 15, 25 (top), 73, 86 (left); Ronald Sheridan, London: 9 (left); Lynda Stone, London: 8 (top), 97, 131; Dr Colin Taylor, Hastings: 14, 22, 24, 27, 30 (middle), 31 (bottom), 32, 44, 45 (bottom), 57, 59 (bottom), 61 (right), 72, 76 (top), 78, 101 (bottom), 103, 105, 110 (bottom), 106, 111; Courtesy of the Texas Memorial Museum, Austin, acc 2257–1: 109.

Thanks also to the Nez Perce Historical Park and Ohio Historical Society.

Portrait of Sígĕsh, an Apache Indian. (Photograph by Edward Curtis, 1903, from *The North American Indian*.)